INTRODUCING
MULTILEVEL
MODELING

ICPSr

ISM   Introducing Statistical Methods

Series editor: Daniel B. Wright, *University of Bristol*

This series provides accessible but in-depth introductions to statistical methods that are not covered in any detail in standard introductory courses. The books are aimed both at the beginning researcher who needs to know how to use a particular technique and the established researcher who wishes to keep up to date with recent developments in statistical data analysis.

Editorial board

INTRODUCING MULTILEVEL MODELING

Ita Kreft
Jan de Leeuw

SAGE Publications

London • Thousand Oaks • New Delhi

First published 1998
Reprinted 2002

SAGE Publications Ltd
6 Bonhill Street
London EC2A 4PU

SAGE Publications Inc
2455 Teller Road
Thousand Oaks, California 91320

SAGE Publications India Pvt Ltd
32, M-Block Market
Greater Kailash-I
New Delhi 110 048

British Library Cataloguing in Publication data

A catalogue record for this book is
available from the British Library

ISBN 0 7619 5140 7
ISBN 0 7619 5141 5 (pbk)

Library of Congress catalog card number 97-62537

Typeset by the Alden Group, Oxford
Printed in Great Britain by The Bath Press, Bath

CONTENTS

PREFACE

This book is for researchers and students in the social sciences with no strong background in statistics and linear algebra. However, we do assume that traditional linear models, such as regression and analysis of variance, are well understood.

The multilevel model presented here is a random coefficient model, with fixed variables and random coefficients. The first chapters introduce the model and its notation, and illustrate it with many examples. Chapter 4 starts with real examples taken from the National Education Longitudinal Study of 1988 (see Appendix). A copy of this data set has been made available on the Internet at ftp://ftp.stat.ucla.edu/pub/faculty/deleeuw/sagebook. The program used for the analyses is MLn, a multilevel program for Windows® written by researchers at the Institute of Education, University of London. In the practical data analysis part of this book the formulas and the notation are replaced by commands used in MLn for fitting different models. The commands in boxes, illustrating the changes in models, are easier to read than formulas, quicker to understand, and do not need an effort on the reader's part to memorize symbols and subscripts, which are always idiosyncrasies of authors. The book is very practical, especially for people planning to use MLn, but is by no means restricted to such users only.

This book is different from others in further respects. It is written with practitioners in mind. Many examples illustrate the possibilities of the models, while explaining the most important features of the output. In the practical part of the book we elaborate on problems and idiosyncrasies of this type of modeling. We do advocate random coefficient models with caution and reservations. Where applicable, we emphasize the trade-offs between using this new model and more traditional models. The contents of this book and the discussion of alternative ways of dealing with hierarchically nested data are based on our own experience in teaching these models, on our experience with analyses of many data sets, and on problems and questions of practitioners in the field discussed in the mailing list for multilevel modeling. (In order to subscribe to this mailing list, send an e-mail with 'join multilevel your name' in the message body to mailbase@mailbase.ac.uk.)

We thank Mahtash Esfandiary (UCLA) and Rien van der Leeden (University of Leiden, The Netherlands) for reading parts of this book. Their comments have greatly improved its readability.

Disclaimers

The reader must realize that this book introduces a statistical method that is of value if and only if several conditions are fulfilled.

The first condition is that the user is aware that this method, just like any other method, can only give answers if the data collection design and the data collected allow such answers. Statistical methods are always imperfect tools for achieving understanding of a complex world.

The second condition is that the user is aware that a method, such as multilevel analysis, is just another strategy for finding patterns in data and for glimpsing the truth. Like any strategy, it may or it may not work.

The third condition is that the user is aware that the multilevel models discussed in this book are based on certain assumptions. If those assumptions are found not to be true, the user can still apply the technique, but standard errors and significance tests in particular must be taken with a large pinch of salt. Of course assumptions, for example that a specific slope is random, can be tested on the sample data. But finding no significant random slope does not mean that this assumption is not true, it is just not significant for this particular sample. It still may be true in 'reality', but that is an answer a statistical model cannot give.

The fourth condition is that the user of multilevel models is aware that statistical models are mathematical models. If the data generation closely resembles the assumptions underlying the statistical model the chances are larger that the conclusions based on the results are close to reality. But reality, in all its complexity, cannot be modeled in a useful way. Complex models may imitate reality well, but will be equally complex, and thus useless tools. Summarizing data in a complex way is not a step forward. Complex statistical models are harder to interpret, and results may be hard to replicate from sample to sample. Complex models are by their nature sensitive to small changes in the system, leading to instability of parameter estimates among models that differ in small ways.

The fifth and last condition is that the user of multilevel models is aware that this tool is useful if data are constructed in the same way as the multilevel model, if a certain knowledge base exists that guides the selection of explanatory variables and random components, and if knowledge of the data is present. Data exploration needs to be done prior to the multilevel modeling stage.

Complex models, such as multilevel models, may be more realistic models, but they are not recommended by the authors of this book for data exploration. We also do not recommend the fitting of extensive models. Large models are models with many explanatory variables, measured at all levels of the hierarchy, and/or models that include all possible cross-level interactions among variables of different levels.

In this book small models are fitted, and explanatory variables are selected based on knowledge of the data and existing theory.

1 INTRODUCTION

1.1 Introduction

This chapter is a short overview of multilevel modeling, its use, its history and its implementation in different software packages. Its usefulness is illustrated with several examples from different research fields. New concepts that play an important role in discussing this new model for the analysis of hierarchically nested data are introduced. The chapter ends with a brief historical overview and a list of available books and software packages.

1.1.1 Hierarchies, micro and macro levels

Hierarchical data structures are very common in the social and behavioral sciences. Individuals can be in various types of groups. There are variables describing individuals, as well as variables describing groups. For instance, data collected on students in schools may contain variables that describe students, such as socio-economic status, attitudes toward homework, gender and ethnicity, as well as variables that describe schools, such as sector (private or public) and type of school, as defined by their student body. School effectiveness researchers collecting such data want to analyze their data at both levels, in order to find the influence on student achievement of the individual student, as well as of the school. The school data example shows the need for techniques that can simultaneously handle measurements made at different levels of a hierarchy.

Multilevel models are developed for analyzing hierarchically structured data. Before elaborating on these models, more must be said about hierarchies. A hierarchy consists of lower-level observations nested within higher level(s). Examples include students nested within schools, employees nested within firms, or repeated measurements nested within persons. The lowest-level measurements are said to be at the *micro level*; all higher-level measurements at the *macro level*. Macro levels are often referred to as *groups*, or more officially as *contexts*. Hence the name *contextual models* for models analyzing data obtained at micro and macro levels. Contextual models can have as few as two levels, as in the case of students (micro level) nested within school classes (macro level); or more than two, for example students nested within classes nested within schools. Many more levels can be thought of, such as students nested within classes, classes nested within schools or neighborhoods, schools nested within states, countries, etc. Once you know that hierarchies exist, you see them everywhere.

1.1.2 Multilevel models

Analysis models that contain variables measured at different levels of the hierarchy are known as *multilevel models*. In multilevel models there is the notion that separate (first-level) linear models for each context should be fitted. Usually each group has the same explanatory variables and the same outcome, but with different regression coefficients. The models are linked together by a second-level model, in which the regression coefficients of the first-level models are regressed on the second-level explanatory variables.

The character of the second-level linking model determines the nature of the model for the complete data. There are several possibilities, starting with no linkage at all, simply specifying a single regression model for each context. Although this is a natural way of handling hierarchically structured or grouped data, it does not add anything new from a statistical point of view. The same holds when the first-level regression coefficients are treated as response variables at the group level in a second step, as is done in 'slopes-as-outcomes' analysis (Burstein *et al.*, 1978). Statistically, in such an analysis the regressions within groups and between groups are not connected with each other. They are indeed separate analyses. In the unlinked as well as in the linked model, the regression coefficients are fixed, not random. The model for the complete data is at most a *varying coefficients model*, where the term just explains how things are: each group is analyzed separately and has its own set of regression coefficients.

The idea of separate regression analyses within each group, followed by regressing first-level regression coefficients on second-level explanatory variables alone, is not sufficient for specifying a multilevel model. It is essential to realize that multilevel models involve a statistical integration of the different models specified at the levels of interest. The simplest integration takes place in the *random coefficients model*, where the first-level regression coefficients are treated as random variables at the second level. This means that a first-level regression coefficient is viewed as 'originating' from a probability distribution. The most important parameters of this distribution, the mean and variance, are among the set of parameters being estimated in the multilevel model. Adding second-level explanatory variables to the random coefficient model makes it more general, and, most of the time, more useful. Such models are commonly called *multilevel models*.

In this book the words 'group' and 'context' are used interchangeably to indicate second- (or higher-) level units in hierarchical data structures. To avoid any confusion, note that 'group' does not refer to the concept of group or treatment group, as used in experimental psychology. 'Group' refers to a *natural* grouping, such as a school or an industry. The word 'context' is used for the same thing and is not meant to specify the much broader concept familiar from sociology. In the next section, the ubiquity of hierarchically nested data, and their implications for the choice of analysis technique, will be illustrated with examples.

1.2 Examples

In this section we discuss several examples from a variety of areas where data have a hierarchically nested structure. The first example is concerned with data on workers nested within industries. It shows that different analyses executed at different levels of the hierarchy do not necessarily lead to the same conclusions. The concept dependency of observations in the same context is discussed. In the second example the data are on students nested within school classes. These examples are followed by several others that illustrate the many areas where multilevel models can be applied.

1.2.1 Income of workers in industry

The first example is from Kreft *et al.* (1995). Data were collected on workers in 12 different industries. Individual-level variables are educational level as the explanatory variable, and income as the response variable. The type of industry, as well as the distinction between public and private industries, are the second-level variables. An analysis with these data, executed at the level of individual workers, shows a positive relationship between educational level and income: the higher the educational level, the higher the personal income. An analysis executed at the higher level, the industry level, with the 12 industries as observations, shows a surprisingly opposite result. A negative relationship shows up between education and income. The higher the average educational level of an industry, the lower the average income of workers in that industry. Universities and colleges are a good example.

The industry-level analysis uses aggregated measurements, such as the mean educational level of the industry, as the explanatory variable and mean income as the response variable. The example shows that analyses executed at different levels of the hierarchy do not necessarily produce the same results. That aggregated measurements analyzed at higher levels of the hierarchy can produce results different from the original individual results has been known since Robinson (1950). This type of aggregation bias has become known as the *Robinson effect*. If in our industry example educational level has a positive effect on income if the unit of analysis is the individual, and a negative effect on income if the unit of analysis is the industry, the logical conclusion is that the variable 'education' measures different things, depending on the unit of analysis. It also shows the need for an analysis model that treats both levels simultaneously, since both levels show important results, which are not unrelated.

Our example also shows another feature of hierarchically nested data. People in the same industry are more alike than people who work in different industries. The extent of homogeneity of industries can be measured by industry characteristics, but more generally by an intra-class correlation.[1] If this intra-class correlation is high, groups are homogeneous and/or very different from each other. This is shown in our analysis results, where educational level explains income far better for workers in the public indus-tries than for workers in the private industries. In general, it is true that if this intra-class correlation is low, groups are only slightly different from each other. If the intra-class correlation is so low that it is equal to zero, no group differences exist for the variables of interest. People within the same group are as different from each other on these variables as people across groups are. A zero intra-class correlation means that clustering of the data has no consequences for the relationship between the variables of interest, and can be subsequently ignored in analyses. By assuming an intra-class correlation, and modeling this correlation, the nested structure of the data is taken into account. Ignoring an intra-class correlation has consequences for the reliability of the results, but only if this correlation is significant and substantial; see, for example, Cochran (1977).

1.2.2   Drug prevention research

The next example in this section is from drug prevention research (Kreft, 1994). In drug prevention research the concern is how effective prevention programs are for teenagers in high school. The treatments are drug preven-tion programs. The objects of measurement and of interest are students. The variables are measured at different levels of the hierarchy – the school level, the class level, and the student level. The schools are randomly sampled, and classes can be considered as a random sample of all possible classes of a certain type, where type depends on the school from which the classes are sampled. The measurements are individual risk factors, such as psychological factors, academic success or failure, and the level of poverty. At the school or class level other risk factors are present, such as the extent of drug use in the school and the type of neighborhood in which the school is located.

In the literature on drug prevention, an interaction effect is assumed between individual risk factors and the type of drug prevention program – but also between school risk factors and individual risk factors. Many hypothesized effects can be found in the literature on drug prevention that mention relations between context and student characteristics. In the lan-guage of multilevel analysis these relations are called cross-level interactions, because the relation crosses the school level and student level. It is expected that certain individuals, such as high-risk students, are more stimulated in certain environments, while other contexts may prevent them from using drugs. For testing such research hypotheses we need an analysis model that not only takes the nested structure of the data into account, but also estimates cross-level interactions.

1.2.3   School effectiveness research

A third example of research that considers both levels of the hierarchy as crucially important can be found in school and teacher effectiveness research.

The objects of interest and measurement are schools and teachers, as well as students. Researchers are interested in how the organizational structure of schools influences the performance of students, or how teacher characteristics such as experience, IQ, or teaching style have an impact on student learning, over and above the influence of students' own attitude and aptitude. Classical examples of such analysis are Cronbach and Webb (1975), Burstein et al. (1978), and Aitkin and Longford (1986).

Given that different teachers or different schools can be considered as different treatments, by analogy with experimental psychology, analysis of covariance (ANCOVA) is the analysis technique most often used. But this technique has problems when used in this context, and given the most important research questions in this field. Modeling the context is possible, but context-specific characteristics cannot be modeled directly. Questions answerable by ANCOVA, such as 'Do schools differ?' are not the most important questions in school effectiveness research. More important is the answer to the question 'Why do schools differ?', which is beyond the power of an ANCOVA analysis to answer.

Further examples are: 'What characteristic of a teacher, or school organization, has an effect on individual student performance?'; 'Are smaller schools more effective than large ones for specific individuals?'; 'Is the private school better than the public school for all students, and if so, what characteristics make private schools better?'; and 'What are the effects of school size on specific groups of students, such as high-risk students, or boys versus girls?'. Research questions that ask about the effect of a specific environment (the size of a school) on a specific type of student (high-risk versus low-risk students, or boys versus girls), need specific analysis techniques to answer them. A technical problem of ANCOVA is that it does not correct for intra-class correlation. ANCOVA has been developed for experimental, randomized groups, where observations are assumed to be independent replications of one another. In real-life groups shared experiences cause dependence of observations in the same context.

1.2.4 Clinical therapy

Another field where multilevel analysis would be useful is in clinical psychology, especially in the evaluation of group therapy research. In group therapy the type of therapy is an effect under the control of the researcher, but the group dynamics is not. Therapy groups are, at the outset, as much alike as chance can make them by randomly assigning clients to therapy groups, but they change over time. The interactions within each group depend on the dynamics of the group, which develops over time in unpredictable directions.

If the two types of group therapy administered are directive intervention and non-directive intervention, groups within the same treatment can become different, especially under the non-directive intervention treatment.

The behavior of each client starts to reflect the type of therapy as well as the specific dynamics that develops in the client's therapy group. The interaction between group members makes clients in the same group more alike than clients in different groups. Consequently, the observations of group members can no longer be considered statistically independent.

Let us consider the problems that arise if we take a traditional approach to analyzing these data. The common approach would be again to use fixed effects ANCOVA with pre-test level of psychological adjustment as the covariate and post-test level of psychological adjustment as the response variable. Therapy groups are nested within treatments, either directive or non-directive intervention. Application of ANCOVA ignores the intra-class correlation that develops over time, leading to an underestimation of the error variance of the estimated coefficients. Groups are nested within one of the two treatments, and although groups start out equal, each develops different processes, not under the control of the experimenter. The group dynamics cannot be modeled in a traditional ANCOVA model, nor can characteristics of the therapist. Hence a new model is needed that takes care of the dependency of observations within groups, and models differences between groups by means of macro-level characteristics, such as different approaches by therapists and different group dynamics. Section 1.2.8 discusses a special case.

1.2.5 Growth curve analysis

Groups are not necessarily always groups of individuals, nested in some sort of natural social context. In multilevel analysis individuals can be the macro level, instead of the micro level. Consider the case where the data consist of repeated measurements on individuals. Measurements are said to be nested within individuals and are correlated within the same individual. Here the intra-class correlation measures the degree to which behavior of the same person is more similar to his/her own previous behavior in comparison to behavior of other people. Recent books discussing random coefficient models in repeated measures analysis are Lindsey (1993) and Diggle *et al.* (1994), but the basic multilevel books we discuss in Section 1.5 also have chapters on repeated measures data.

In educational examples, a three-level hierarchy exists when data consist of repeated measurements on students in schools. Repeated measurements make up the first level, nested within students, making up the second level, nested within schools, the third level.

We shall see, in Chapter 5, that the multilevel techniques we discuss in this book can easily deal with repeated measurement data, including unbalanced cases with missing data. This is perhaps one of the most interesting areas of application, although especially in social science research there has always been an emphasis on cross-sectional analysis, as discussed in the previous examples in this section.

1.2.6 Geographical information systems

Spatial statistics is finding more and more applications. Census data, election data, and surveys have always been structured geographically, but only recently have the tools become available to incorporate geographical information in the analysis. Again, multilevel models can be used in an obvious way here. Sites or individuals are nested within geographic regions, and thus the intra-class correlation comes from spatial autocorrelation. A general and comprehensive reference for spatial statistics is the book by Cressie (1991), which also discusses the relationship between kriging and the hierarchical linear model.

Again, multilevel techniques can be easily adapted to spatial situations. To show this, we discuss an example due to McMillan and Berliner (1994). Corn yields in bushels are measured on 3842 farms in Iowa. Farms are classified according to size into three types, but they are also in 88 counties. The model used by McMillan and Berliner is basically a variance components model, with a random component for farms and a random component for counties. The covariance matrix of the county components is then modeled by Markov random field techniques. Classical multilevel analysis as defined in this book would be an alternative, in which county characteristics are used as second-level explanatory variables of the 88 farm-level separate regression coefficients. Thus adjacent farms in different counties are not spatially correlated, but farms in the same county are.

1.2.7 Meta-analysis

In *meta-analysis* the problem is to summarize the outcomes of different studies, in which each study produces an estimate of the size of an effect or difference. In many cases individual observations on which the results of the studies are based can no longer be used. They are lost or otherwise unavailable. In quite a few meta-analytic studies some of the outcomes are proportions, others are means, some may be correlations, and so on. We can still apply a form of multilevel analysis, because the groups, which are the collected studies or articles in this case, are independent. Of course individual observations are lost, but standard errors of the estimates are reported by researchers in these studies. These standard errors are used *as if* they are the results of the first step of a multilevel analysis, and the second step is the meta-analysis at the article or group level. For more detail, see Bryk and Raudenbush (1992).

1.2.8 Twin and family studies

This example is different from previous ones, because the groups are small. In twin studies, we have a number of groups of size two. We may have many groups, but they are all very small. There is very little hope that we can estimate a model within each group, because we have only two observations. The statistical stability has to come from the number of groups.

The following example is related to the hotly debated 'IQ controversy', which discusses the notorious pseudo-question of whether IQ is inherited or environmentally determined (nature or nurture). Suppose we have IQ data for monozygotic and dizygotic twin pairs. If IQ has a genetic component, then obviously the within-group correlation for monozygotic and dizygotic pairs will be different, and if IQ has a high genetic component, the within-group correlation for monozygotic pairs will be large. In fact, under the usual and unrealistic assumptions, it will be equal to the heritability of IQ. Again, this makes the example special, because we have small groups of two, but also these small groups have a high intra-class correlation. In a multilevel analysis we can use separate variables for the individuals in the pairs, and variables which the members of the pairs have in common.

A similar example, which is also of interest in the social and behavioral sciences, concerns data on married couples. Again, these data come in groups of size two. Observe that in the twin data the members of the group are exchangeable; it does not matter which twin we call A and which twin we call B. In marriage data there is much less symmetry within groups, because one group member is the husband and one member is the wife – a distinction that cannot be ignored yet in present-day society.

1.3 Summarizing discussion and definitions

In the previous sections several concepts and terms have been introduced, all important in understanding the analysis of hierarchically structured data. For a better understanding of the subsequent chapters, definitions of the terms *contextual models, intra-class correlation, random and fixed coefficients, shrinkage, prediction,* and *cross-level interaction* are summarized below.

1.3.1 Contextual models

Traditionally, contextual models are defined as regression models containing two types of variables: individual-level variables and aggregated context variables, such as group means or medians. For instance, data are collected on students, nested within school classes, where students' achievement is predicted by their socio-economic status (SES), but also by the mean SES of the school class to which they belong. The variable SES is used twice, once as an individual student variable and once as an aggregated school class characteristic. In the literature, only a regression analysis with such an aggregated context variable (mean SES in this example) is considered a contextual model (Duncan *et al.*, 1966).

In this book the concept of the *contextual model* is extended and used for any linear regression model that contains lower-level variables and higher-level characteristics that are aggregated or globally measured. Global characteristics are defined (see Lazarsfeld and Menzel, 1969) as variables that measure characteristics of the context directly, instead of using aggregates of variables that are measured over individuals. Any type of regression model with individual- and context-level characteristics is referred to as a *contextual model*. Random coefficient models with higher-level variables in the model are in this sense contextual models.

1.3.2 Intra-class correlation

Intra-class correlation is illustrated with an example from school effectiveness research. Students are nested within schools, and both students and schools are the objects of interest and of observation. Observations that are close in time and/or space are likely to be more similar than observations far apart in time and/or space. Therefore, students in the same school are more alike than students in different schools, due to shared experiences, shared environment, etc. The sharing of the same context is a likely cause of dependency among observations.

The intra-class correlation is a measure of the degree of dependence of individuals. The more individuals share common experiences due to closeness in space and/or time, the more they are similar, or to a certain extent, duplications of each other. The highest degree of dependency can be found between the two observations of a monozygotic twin, or children born and raised in the same family. Another well-known example of dependent observations concerns repeated measurements on the same person.

To acknowledge the existence of an intra-class correlation is important because it changes the error variance in traditional linear regression models. This error variance represents the effect of all omitted variables and measurement errors, under the assumption that these errors are unrelated. In traditional linear models omitted variables are assumed to have a random and not a structural effect, a debatable assumption in data that contain clustered observations. For example, in a school effectiveness study, structural influences of unmeasured variables can be school climate or peer pressure. The degree of covariance in the error terms of individuals sharing the same school or class is expressed in the intra-class correlation coefficient.

Intra-class correlation, generally indicated by ρ, can be summarized in several ways. Above it is described as the degree to which individuals share common experiences due to closeness in space and/or time. It can also be called a measure of group homogeneity. More formally, with data having a two-level hierarchical structure, it is defined as the proportion of the variance in the outcome variable that is between the second-level units. In one way or another, these descriptions and definitions of intra-class correlation refer to the existence of intra-class or intra-context dependency. This means that if intra-class correlation is present, as it may be when we are dealing with clustered data, the assumption of independent observations in the traditional linear model is violated.

— if all assumptions are correct, α should be .05

Table 1.1 The inflation of the alpha level of 0.05 in the presence of intra-class correlation (Barcikowski, 1981, p. 270)

N_i	ρ		
	0.01	0.05	0.20
10	0.06	0.11	0.28
25	0.08	0.19	0.46
50	0.11	0.30	0.59
100	0.17	0.43	0.70

Type I error rates

The values in the body of the table are the observed alpha levels; N_i denotes the number of observations within a group

A striking illustration of the effect of this violation is the increase in the probability of a type I error (the alpha level), in the literature associated with the presence of intra-class correlation. Thirty students in the same school class are no longer 30 independent observations, but less than that. How much less depends on the degree of similarity between the group members or the homogeneity of the group. The strength of the intra-class correlation determines how many independent observations there really are. Since tests of significance lean heavily on the number of independent observations, the existence of intra-class correlation makes the test of significance in traditional linear models too liberal (see Barcikowski, 1981). Barcikowski shows that in most applications of analysis of variance, the standard errors of the parameter estimates will be underestimated. A small intra-class correlation (say, $\rho = 0.01$) can inflate the alpha level substantially, as is shown in Table 1.1, which is based on analysis of variance (ANOVA). It shows that for large groups ($N_j = 100$), a small intra-class correlation of $\rho = 0.01$ inflates the type I error rate from the assumed 0.05 to an observed 0.17. For small groups ($N_j = 10$), a large intra-class correlation of 0.20 enhances the observed alpha level to 0.28 instead of the assumed 0.05. In general, the rule applies that a small intra-class correlation in large groups has effects on the inflation of the alpha level similar to those of a large intra-class correlation in a small group. Similarly, a small intra-class correlation may hardly affect the alpha level in small groups, while it increases the alpha level in a significant way in large groups.

The differential effect of the intra-class correlation follows the usual pattern of traditional correlation coefficients: small correlations not significant in small samples, are significant in large samples. For more details on this topic we refer to Barcikowski (1981) and Cochran (1977).

1.3.3 Fixed versus random coefficients

There is a lot of confusion associated with the terms 'random' and 'fixed'. In the context of linear modeling, the terms apply to three different entities:

random or fixed effects, random or fixed variables, and random or fixed coefficients.

Fixed and random effects are concepts commonly used in experimental research where treatments and treatment groups are involved, and data are analyzed using analysis of variance. A factor, defining different treatments, is said to have a fixed effect if all possible treatments in which the researcher is interested are present in the experiment. A random effect is attributed to a factor defining treatments that can be considered a sample from the universe of all relevant treatments. Classical references are Scheffé (1956) and Wilk and Kempthorne (1955). For instance, consider a thoroughly controlled laboratory experiment, where the effect of a certain drug is evaluated. A treatment group is given the drug, and a control group is given a placebo. Some relevant measure is taken as the response variable. Clearly, the two treatments form a fixed factor, since by the nature of this experiment they are the only two possible treatments. In quasi-experimental research using real-life groups, the assumption of fixed treatments can almost never be made. The earlier example from school effectiveness research illustrates this. Experimentation with different forms of drug prevention program uses existing groups, such as schools. These groups are not equal to each other, like randomized groups are. Schools are just a random sample from all possible schools. An effect of a drug prevention program in a certain school has to be defined as random instead of fixed, and thus treatment effects have to be viewed as random instead of fixed effects.

The distinction between fixed and random effects is useful, because it has consequences for inferences that can be made and for the generalization of the results. For instance, fixed effects only allow inferences made regarding the treatments used in the experiment. The effects are assumed to be 'constant' and without measurement error. In random effects models, as in the example with the schools, inferences are extended beyond the schools in the sample. The intent is to generalize to the population of schools and not only to the schools in the treatments. The effects are not assumed to be constant, but to be slightly different, or measured with sampling error. This is a direct result of the fact that a sample of schools is used, and that we want to generalize to the population. We expect more or less different results if the 'experiment' is repeated and another sample of schools is examined.

The same concepts, 'constant' and 'random', are used as prefixes for variables. Again the idea of measurement error applies here. Randomness, as applied to variables, is not a concept that is relevant for random coefficient models. Random coefficient models assume fixed variables. Random variables are only discussed here to clarify the distinction between random variables and random coefficients. Fixed and random variables are concepts known in statistical theory. A loose, but for our purpose sufficient, definition of a random variable is a variable with values selected from a probability distribution. Thus, a random variable has an expected value (the 'mean') and a variance (which may be either known or unknown). In general, we assume that a random variable is measured with error and differs from measurement to measurement. IQ is an example. A person's intelligence can be tested several times under the same conditions, with a different result each time. A fixed variable is a variable with values that are known, fixed quantities. Gender is an example. Each time a person is measured we assume that the same gender will appear. Predictor variables in traditional regression analysis and the design variables in analysis of variance are generally considered to be fixed variables, specifying the 'fixed' design of the analysis. But in models for linear structural relations analysis variables are considered to be random. Again, loosely formulated, in fixed variables the interest is in the value of the variables as it appears. In random variables the interest is mainly in the parameters defining the corresponding probability distributions. Throughout this book the explanatory variables are assumed to be fixed.

The idea of fixed and random coefficients is a new concept introduced here in relation to random coefficient models. The concept applies to the characteristics of the linear model parameters. In ordinary regression models the parameter estimates that specify the regression line are intercept and slope(s). Traditionally, these coefficients are assumed to be fixed, and the values are estimated from the data. Random coefficients are coefficients of which the values are assumed to be distributed as a probability function. In a multilevel modeling framework, for instance, the coefficients of the first-level regression model are treated as random. Sometimes the interest of the researcher is in the expectation of these parameters, sometimes in the variance of these random coefficients, sometimes in both. For instance, a random coefficient for the slope is estimated in two parts. One part is the value for the overall slope, estimated over all individuals, irrespective of the group to which they belong. The second part is the slope variance, which represents a deviation of each group from the overall slope. Multilevel models, as in random coefficients models, allow groups to deviate from the mean solution, either in the intercept or the slope(s). In this book we will elaborate on these models in their various forms.

1.3.4 Cross-level interactions

Cross-level interactions are defined as interactions between variables measured at different levels in hierarchically structured data. An example is the interaction between context and student, such as between an individual student characteristic like gender, and teacher characteristics like attitude towards gender issues. Cronbach and Webb (1975) were the first to mention cross-level interaction in the educational research literature.

The hypothesis tested by Cronbach and Webb was that effective teachers were only effective with certain types of students, and not necessarily effective with all students. If certain teachers are, for instance, more effective with bright students than with others, this means that the relationship between an individual student's aptitude and achievement is strengthened by such a teacher. We say that such a teacher has a meritocratic teaching style. If, on the other hand, a teacher is more effective with slow learners, the relationship between aptitude and achievement may be weakened. We say that the teacher has an egalitarian teaching style. The first type of teacher widens the gap between high and low performers, while the second type of teacher narrows this gap. In the educational literature this is called an aptitude–treatment interaction or ATI. Defining students as the micro level and teachers as the macro level, such a cross-level interaction is a micro–macro interaction. The stronger the micro–macro interaction, the stronger the effect of the teacher on that specific type of student, either in a positive or in a negative way.

1.3.5 Prediction

Regression models, no matter whether they have fixed coefficients or random coefficients, are tools for *prediction* or tools for *description*. Prediction can be either actual prediction or virtual prediction. Actual prediction can be checked against reality to find out afterwards how good the prediction was. In the case of virtual prediction the investigator assumes a relationship which cannot be checked against reality. For instance, the researcher predicts, based on a regression equation, that if the socio-economic status of the parents is increased by one point, and the other explanatory variables are kept constant, then the school achievement of the child will increase by 40 standard aptitude test (SAT) points. It is clear that these types of thought experiment can sometimes be pretty far removed from what is feasible or relevant in the real world. Moreover, there is no way to show that these predictions are actually true or false without extending them to real predictions.

Regression models can also be used to simply describe relationships between variables. We can compute that the mean SAT of children in particular SES classes is approximately a linear function of the SES values. We can be more precise, and describe the within-class variance, the variance 'due to regression'. Again, description is of limited value if it does not result in predictions that can be verified in experiments or replications. Statistics tries to take over the role of repeating an experiment. The assumption is that if the same experiment were done a hundred times the results would be a bit different each time. To be more precise, it is assumed that 95% of the time the observed value will be no further than two standard errors away from the true value. But again these hypothetical replications are thought experiments which may be impossible to realize.

The purpose of multilevel analysis, in this context, is to be able to make better predictions, as well as to describe accurately the relationship that is present. We have to realize that a multilevel analysis generally improves the description by introducing additional parameters, the variance and covariance components that describe the correlation between first-level units. But introducing additional parameters comes with a price. It means that the regression coefficients can no longer be estimated as precisely as before. In fact precision is given up for a diminution of the bias in the estimates. Throughout statistics a common theme is 'trade-off'. Here that trade-off is between increasing the number of parameters and decreasing the precision with which the parameters of interest can be estimated. If too many parameters are estimated in one single model, precision suffers so much that the results are rendered useless for prediction.

1.3.6 Shrinkage estimation and borrowing strength

Random coefficient models are compromises between modeling each context separately with its own model and modeling all contexts simultaneously with the same model. The first alternative is wasteful, in terms of the many para-meters that need to be estimated. The number of parameters is so large because at least three are needed for each context: one for the intercept, one for the slope and one for the error variance. Moreover, the need for separate analyses for separate contexts contradicts our knowledge that groups are related to each other. For instance, all contexts are schools within the same educational system. The second alternative, one single model for all contexts together, is too parsimonious in many cases, that is to say, it does not have enough parameters for a useful description.

The trade-off here is a very familiar one in statistics. We can choose between models with a small number of parameters (relative to the number of observations) and models with a large number of parameters. If we choose the smaller number of parameters, the coefficients can be estimated with a great deal of precision, but at the likely cost of bias. Precision because we have a small sampling variance, and bias because this variance is around an incorrect value. Conversely, with a large number of parameters, we have smaller bias, but also smaller precision, and we see large standard errors around the correct value. Both extremes are undesirable, and we have to find a compromise in the middle somewhere. This is discussed in many places, for instance in de Leeuw (1994).

There is another way of looking at this, which has been discussed at great length in a recent National Research Council (1992) report; compare also Draper (1995). Each individual study or group may be too small to give a precise idea about the processes that are going on. But by pooling schools or studies, we 'borrow strength' from other schools or studies to obtain a more powerful analysis. Of course this idea (which is surprisingly general) only works if schools are related in interesting ways.

The effect of borrowing strength is invariably that individual estimates, for a single school or study, are 'shrunk' to the overall solution. Results of shrinkage are most noticeable if the number of observations in a single con-text is small. The parameter estimates computed by random coefficient models are a compromise between the estimates over the total population summed over all contexts, and the estimates for each context calculated separately. Clearly the idea of borrowing strength is also at the very basis of meta-analysis.

1.4 Brief history

In this section we make some remarks on the history of multilevel models. It completes and improves on the historical remarks given in de Leeuw and Kreft (1986). The key papers in various areas are summarized in order to show what their relationships are. In particular, we concentrate on review papers and textbooks. The purpose of this section is to show that developments similar to those in educational statistics are going on elsewhere, or have been going on. The section gives an entry into the various specialized literatures as well.

Tools developed in one area can often also be used in other areas. One of the useful functions of statistics as an academic discipline is to coordinate and document data analysis developments in different disciplines. This overview will show that multilevel models are a conglomerate of known models such as variance component models (Section 1.4.1), random coefficient models in econometrics (1.4.2), variable and changing coefficient models (1.4.3 and 1.4.4), the analysis of panel data (1.4.5), growth curve models (1.4.6), and Bayesian and empirical Bayesian estimation methods (1.4.7). The concepts of moderator variables (1.4.8) and slopes as outcomes (1.4.9) are also related to multilevel models.

1.4.1 Variance components

Variance component analysis (and mixed model analysis) has a long and complicated history, which is discussed in considerable detail in the book by Searle et al. (1992). The first use of the technique was in astronomy by Airy (1861). But, of course, the seminal work was by Fisher (1918; 1925). The distinction between fixed effects and random effects, and the birth of the mixed model, can be dated to the work of Eisenhart (1947). Between 1950 and 1970 the field was dominated by the Henderson (1953) methods for estimating variance components, and around 1970 the computational revolution made it possible to compute maximum likelihood estimates (see Hartley and Rao, 1967; Hemmerle and Hartley, 1973; Harville, 1977; Searle, 1979; Thomson, 1980). Since 1970 there has been a lot of emphasis on computation, for which we refer to the excellent review paper by Engel (1990), and some progress toward a deeper understanding of what we mean by an 'analysis of variance'. Two interesting papers on this last topic are by Speed (1987) and Samuels et al. (1991).

1.4.2 Random coefficients

Random coefficient models were proposed in econometrics in the Cowles Commission days by Wald (1947) and by Rubin (1950). The computational revolution made these models also practically relevant, and during the 1970s there were review papers by Rosenberg (1973), Spjøtvoll (1977), and a monograph by Swamy (1971). A bibliography has been published by Johnson (1977; 1980). Recently there have been some attempts to make random coefficient models semiparametric, in the sense that the distribution of the random effects is not assumed to be normal, but is estimated from the data. For the linear case, see Beran and Hall (1992); for the nonlinear case, see Davidian and Gallant (1992).

1.4.3 Variable coefficients

This is a very general class of models. Each individual has her own vector of regression coefficients, which depends on a number of parameters, possibly in a nonlinear way. In this generality the model depends heavily on computational tools such as smoothing. It has been discussed recently by Hastie and Tibshirani (1993), and related to the generalized additive models they discuss in their book (Hastie and Tibshirani, 1990). Observe that the coefficients in these models are fixed.

1.4.4 Changing coefficients

Consider a random coefficient model in which the relation between the response variable and the explanatory variables is a linear regression model, with a different vector of regression coefficients for each time point t. In order not to be overwhelmed by the number of parameters, we have to assume a 'second-level' model connecting the vectors of regression coefficients in time. It is usually assumed that the regression coefficients satisfy an autoregressive path model. There has recently been much interest in this model. The literature until 1984 is reviewed by Chow (1984). There is a close relationship with the Kalman filter of control system theory fame.

1.4.5 Panel data

In economics, at least micro-economics, panel data, which follow a number of individuals in time, have received a great deal of attention. We refer to the review paper by Chamberlain (1984), and the books by Hsiao (1986) and Dielman (1992). The models are usually variable coefficient regression models, sometimes with random coefficients. In many cases they are fairly straightforward mixed models or variance component models (Wansbeek, 1980).

1.4.6 Growth curves and repeated measurements

Growth curve models have been studied in biometry since Wishart. The key paper here is Pothoff and Roy (1964). They introduce a multivariate linear model which can actually be written as a balanced version of the usual two-level model without the random component at the second level. Rao (1965) linked growth curves with random coefficient modeling. The multivariate analysis of variance (MANOVA) approach to growth curve modeling, and the related modeling of repeated measurements, are discussed by Geisser (1980) and Timm (1980). The relation with multilevel models is discussed in detail in Strenio *et al.* (1983) and Jennrich and Schluchter (1986).

1.4.7 Bayesian linear models and empirical Bayes estimation

There is a strong formal relationship between multilevel modeling and the Bayesian analysis of the linear model discussed extensively by Lindley, Smith, Leamer, Zellner and others (Lindley and Smith, 1972; Smith, 1973). We call the relationship 'formal' because there is nothing inherently Bayesian about assuming coefficients to be random. The models can be interpreted equally well as frequentist mixture models.

The use of shrinkage estimators in linear models can also be motivated from mean square error considerations, using the basic James–Stein theory. Classical papers by Efron and Morris (1975) and Morris (1983) explain the data analysis aspects of shrinkage estimation. The National Research Council (1992) discusses the notion of 'borrowing strength' in considerable detail. The report concentrates on meta-analysis as the main area of application, but the methodological discussion is quite general.

1.4.8 Moderator variables

The concept of a moderator variable is not easily defined. There is a thoughtful review in Baron and Kenny (1986). Velicer (1972) discusses the concept in terms of different regressions in different groups, and in an early paper Saunders (1956) explicitly takes the point of view that regression coefficients in an equation are themselves response variables in a second set of equations.

1.4.9 Slopes as outcomes

'Slopes-as-outcomes' analysis was proposed by Burstein *et al.* (1978) as an alternative to the variance decomposition techniques of Cronbach. A nice historical review of the approach is given in Burstein *et al.* (1989). The technique is two-step ordinary least squares (OLS), but it was quite unclear what the precise statistical model behind the computations was. In a sense, the random coefficients models are one attempt to make the slopes-as-outcomes approach rigorous.

1.5 Further reading

There are three other books on random coefficient regression or multilevel analysis that we are aware of. All three are more advanced than this book, in the sense of requiring a stronger background in statistics, matrix algebra and/or analysis. If you have such a background, then they are excellent material for further reading. As a guide, we provide nutshell reviews of all three books.

Bryk and Raudenbush (1992) is oriented toward educational statistics, and its use in education departments or schools. It presents the multilevel material in the way it is implemented in the program HLM, using mainly the options of that program to discuss variations in the technique. The examples in the text are mostly from education, with a relatively small number of variables. There is not much emphasis on model criticism and on alternative methods of analysis. There are chapters on applications to meta-analysis, in which the variance and covariance components are assumed to be known, and on repeated measures and growth curves. Generally, the book enthusiastically presents a new class of techniques, which are an important step ahead in solving problems of educational and sociological statistics.

Longford (1993) is more technical than the book by Bryk and Raudenbush, with much less emphasis on multilevel modeling and the slopes-as-outcomes approach. As the title of the book indicates, it is about random coefficient models, which are special mixed linear models in which the variance and covariance components derive from random regression coefficients (including intercepts). The treatment of random coefficient models is both thorough and clear, starting with random analysis of covariance, and progressing to categorical and multivariate outcomes.

The book by Goldstein exists in two versions (Goldstein, 1987; 1995). The more recent edition is a major extension of the 1987 book, and supersedes it in all respects. The book treats the general principles of multilevel modeling, and then proceeds to apply these general principles to many of the more common statistical models. Usually relatively few details are given, but the conceptual unity of the various extensions is emphasized again and again. There are chapters on categorical response variables, event history analysis, errors-in-variables and simultaneous equation models, and generalized linear models. It is not an introductory book, or a book reviewing a class of models in detail. It is more like a program for research, reporting the progress so far, and mapping out areas for future development.

1.6 Software

There are, by now, many software tools that can be used to analyze hierarchical data with linear models. Such models are special cases of mixed linear models, and as a consequence they can be analyzed, in principle, with programs that fit mixed linear models. On the other hand, they are rather special types of mixed linear models, and consequently it makes sense to develop special software packages that take the special properties of the model into account. As in the previous section, we will give very brief reviews of the available packages and programs, with some indication of their strong and weak points. A much more extensive comparison of some of the older packages is in the paper by Kreft et al. (1994) and the related report by Kreft et al. (1990).

Throughout this book, we use the package MLn, developed and described by Rasbash et al. (1991). Our reason for selecting MLn is not necessarily that we think it is superior to the other packages (although in some respects it is), but also that it provides a convenient notation to describe data and model manipulation in multilevel analysis. This notation can be used in the same way as mathematical formulas, with the advantage that many people find formulas more difficult to understand than computer instructions of this type. Our book is not, however, a user's guide for MLn. Much better documentation is available for that purpose, such as Woodhouse (1995), Rasbash and Woodhouse (1995), and Prosser et al. (1991).

In this section information is provided on where programs and software can be found on the World Wide Web (if they are free) and where they can be ordered (if they are not).

1.6.1 HLM

In educational statistics, the package HLM plays a special role. In the United States it was adapted, soon after its release, as the 'official' software for educational multilevel analysis. The manual (Bryk et al., 1988) is clearly written, the program has relatively few user options, and is structured along the lines of the slopes-as-outcomes tradition, which is very familiar ground for most educational researchers. The user interface is a relatively simple question-and-answer format, and the program provides some useful tests and descriptive statistics. Further information is available from

http://www.gamma.rug.nl/iechome.html

1.6.2 VARCL

VARCL, written by Longford (1990), is a program for variance component analysis of hierarchical data. VARCL is designed as a program for random coefficient analysis, not as a program for multilevel analysis. Thus the user has to decide for each variable whether the coefficient has a fixed or a random part, but there is no way to create cross-level interactions in a simple way. VARCL uses the scoring method, and has extensions to Poisson and binomial response models. VARCL comes in two flavors. The first version of the program analyzes random slopes and intercepts for models with up to three levels, the second version handles random intercept models with up to nine levels. Further information is available from

http://www.gamma.rug.nl/iechome.html

1.6.3 BMDP5-V

BMDP5-V is a part of the well-known BMDP package. It was written by Jennrich and Schluchter (1986). This program is meant for repeated measures data, that is to say, for balanced designs with relatively few observations within each of the second-level units. It can be used for other forms of multilevel analysis as well, but only after the user makes quite complicated command files. BMDP5-V can choose between various techniques and algorithms. It also has various options to model the dispersion of the second-level residuals. Information is available from

http://www.spss.com/software/science/Bmdp/

1.6.4 MLn

MLn was developed by the Multilevel Project at the Institute of Education, University of London. A very useful feature of MLn is that it is integrated with the general-purpose statistics package NANOSTAT, which means a lot of data manipulation and elementary analysis is possible within the program's shell. MLn can analyze up to 15 levels and various crossed and nested structures. It has a macro language, which is used, for instance, to write modules for categorical outcomes. You can read more about MLn at

http://www.ioe.ac.uk/multilevel/

1.6.5 PROC MIXED

PROC MIXED is the mixed model analysis component of the SAS statistics system. It is comparable in options and possibilities to BMDP5-V. For further information, see

http://www.sas.com/

1.6.6 MIXOR and MIXREG

The MIXOR and MIXREG programs were written by Don Hedeker (Hedeker and Gibbons, 1993a; 1993b). The theory is described in Hedeker's dissertation (Hedeker, 1989) and in Hedeker and Gibbons (1994). MIXOR does multilevel analysis with an ordinal outcome variable, MIXREG does multilevel analysis with autocorrelated errors. Binaries for PC and Macintosh, and manuals, can be obtained from

http://www.uic.edu/~hedeker/mixdos.html

The programs fit two-level models, using Newton–Raphson procedures.

1.7 Summary

Many new concepts regarding multilevel analyses are introduced in this introductory chapter. We show that some old concepts acquire a new meaning, such as contextual models and micro/macro level. Other concepts are specific and new, such as random and fixed coefficients and intra-class correlation. Several real-life examples show the usefulness of multilevel models, especially for testing new theories about human behavior in context, for instance by fitting cross-level interactions. The brief historical overview of multilevel modeling shows that the ideas of such models are and were applied in many different fields of research, and for different purposes. The discussion of the latest developments in software show that multilevel techniques are becoming more and more accessible and easier to use.

Note

1 The intra-class correlation is the proportion of the total variance that is between groups.

2 OVERVIEW OF CONTEXTUAL MODELS

2.1 Introduction

In this chapter we discuss the important differences in the way traditional regression models decompose variation present in the data. The total regression model allows only individual variation to be modeled, while an aggregated model does the opposite and models only variation among contexts. Traditional contextual models, the Cronbach model, the ANCOVA model and the various multilevel models decompose the variation in the data into a within and a between part, but each in their own way. To illustrate the effects of this decomposition, results of an analysis with a small sample from the National Education Longitudinal Study of 1988 (NELS-88) data set are presented and discussed. In Section 2.10 we discuss briefly the commands that are used to fit the models with MLn.

2.2 Models

In this chapter we discuss a number of variations on the ordinary linear model and on OLS regression – variations that have been suggested to deal with hierarchically nested data. They vary from *total* or *pooled* regression, which completely ignores the between-group variation, to *aggregate* regression, which completely ignores the within-group variation. And, on another dimension, they vary from separate regressions for each group, with separate sets of regression parameters, to a single regression with only one set of parameters.

In many cases, however, it makes sense to take the group structure into account more explicitly. Forms of regression analysis, in which both individual- and group-level variables are used, are known as *contextual analyses*. In contextual analysis group membership is not neglected. The units of observation are treated as members of certain groups, because the research interest is in individuals as well as in their contexts.

In contextual analysis techniques the free parameters of the linear model are estimated based on the following model, where y is the response variable, and x the explanatory variable at the individual level, and z is the explanatory variable at the context level.[1] The subscript i is for individual, and j is for context. The model is

$$\underline{y}_{ij} = a + bx_{ij} + cz_j + \underline{\varepsilon}_{ij}. \tag{2.1}$$

The ε_{ij} are disturbances, which are *centered, homoscedastic* and *independent*. This means they have expectation zero and constant variance σ^2. Generally, of course, there may be more than one explanatory variable on both levels.

Model (2.1) can be written in a slightly different way, that more clearly shows its structure. We write

$$y_{ij} = a_j + bx_{ij} + \varepsilon_{ij}, \tag{2.2a}$$

$$a_j = a + cz_j. \tag{2.2b}$$

Equation (2.2b) shows that the contextual models of equation (2.1) are *varying intercept models*, i.e. regression models for each group which are linked because they have the same slope b and the same error variance σ^2. They differ, however, in their intercepts. The different contextual models we discuss in this chapter specify the relationship between the varying intercepts and the group-level variables in different ways.

2.3 Data

In this chapter we illustrate several analyses by using a subset of NELS-88. The data were collected by the National Center for Education Statistics of the US Department of Education. They constitute the first in a series of longitudinal measurements on students, starting in the eighth grade. The data consist of approximately 1000 schools (800 public and 200 private schools) in the United States that enroll eighth-grade students. More than 20 000 students across the United States participated in the base year study. The sample represents the nation's eighth-grade population, totaling about 3 million eighth-graders in more than 38 000 schools in spring 1988. In this chapter we use a small subset selected from the NELS-88 data for illustrative purposes. In later chapters the entire sample is used and more realistic analyses are discussed.

Our subset consists of 10 handpicked schools from the 1003 schools in the NELS-88 data set. There are 260 students in this subset, a tiny fraction of the original 21 580 students in the full data set. The variables in the model are the number of hours of homework (which is a micro-level variable) and the score on a math test; the former will serve as our explanatory variable, the latter as our response variable. Thus we wish to find out whether and to what extent amount of homework ('HomeWork') causes or predicts achievement in math ('MathAchievement').[2] The school-level characteristic ('Public') of interest is the sector to which schools belong; public schools are coded 1 and private coded 0. The schools are picked from the two ends of the continuum, with strong positive and strong negative relationships between math score and amount of homework. Another reason for our selection is that the school regression lines show interesting variation. The majority of schools in the NELS-88 data set show a positive relationship between time devoted to

Table 2.1   Ten selected schools from NELS-88:
within-school means

School	Size	Math mean	Homework mean
1	23	45.8	1.39
2	20	42.2	2.35
3	24	53.2	1.83
4	22	43.6	1.64
5	22	49.7	0.86
6	20	46.4	1.15
7	67	62.8	3.30
8	21	49.6	2.10
9	21	46.3	1.33
10	20	47.8	1.60

in move.txt file

homework and math achievement. A description of our 10 schools is given in
Tables 2.1 and 2.2. Table 2.1 gives the mean math score (number correct) and
amounts of homework (in hours per week), Table 2.2 the variances,
covariances and correlations. The variables are described in more detail in
the Appendix. Before discussing the analysis results of different models, we
elaborate a little on the crucial distinction between parameter estimates
within and between groups (or contexts).

Table 2.2   Ten selected schools from NELS-88:
within-school dispersions and correlations

School	Dispersion		Correlation
A	55.2	−4.24	−0.52
	−4.24	1.19	
B	65.1	−4.65	−0.45
	−4.65	1.63	
C	126.3	9.62	0.77
	9.62	1.22	
D	94.1	11.9	0.84
	11.9	2.14	
E	69.2	−2.71	−0.43
	−2.71	0.57	
F	17.0	−1.56	−0.48
	−1.56	0.63	
G	31.2	3.24	0.34
	3.24	2.92	
H	101.1	7.94	0.71
	7.94	1.22	
I	86.6	4.61	0.56
	4.61	0.79	
J	120.9	12.3	0.80
	12.3	1.94	

• Var./Covariance
School by
school

2.4   Decomposition of variation

In hierarchically nested data with two levels the variances and covariances of the observed variables can be divided into a between-group and a within-group matrix. This distinction of within and between variation of variables is not entirely straightforward and differs from technique to technique. To explain the definition of regression coefficients in different models we make use of the notion of the correlation ratio. The correlation ratio is the percentage group variance of a variable, which can be explained as follows. Variables used in equations earlier in this book, such as x as an explanatory variable and y as response variable, can be divided into a between- and a within-group part. This induces a corresponding decomposition of the variances as

$$V_T(x) = V_B(x) + V_W(x) \qquad (2.3a)$$

and equally

$$V_T(y) = V_B(y) + V_W(y), \qquad (2.3b)$$

where the indices T, B and W denote total variance, between-group variance, and within-group variance, respectively. Familiar from ANCOVA, the total covariance between variables x and y can be divided in the same way into a within and a between part,

$$C_T(x, y) = C_B(x, y) + C_W(x, y), \qquad (2.3c)$$

where C denotes covariance.

The coefficients for regressions over the total sample b_T, between groups, b_B, and within groups b_W, can be defined by the variances within or between groups, compared to the total variance, as follows:[3]

$$b_T \triangleq \frac{C_T(x, y)}{V_T(x)}, \qquad (2.4a)$$

$$b_B \triangleq \frac{C_B(x, y)}{V_B(x)}, \qquad (2.4b)$$

$$b_W \triangleq \frac{C_W(x, y)}{V_W(x)}. \qquad (2.4c)$$

These coefficients can be related to the correlation ratio η^2, defined for x and y in the following way:

$$\eta^2(x) \triangleq \frac{V_B(x)}{V_T(x)}, \qquad (2.5a)$$

$$\eta^2(y) \triangleq \frac{V_B(y)}{V_T(y)}. \qquad (2.5b)$$

The equations show group variation in the response variable as the percentage of the total variance in y declared between groups. This is at the same time the definition of the intra-class correlation as discussed in Chapter 1.

Also,

$$1 - \eta^2(x) = \frac{V_W(x)}{V_T(x)}, \tag{2.6a}$$

$$1 - \eta^2(y) = \frac{V_W(y)}{V_T(y)}. \tag{2.6b}$$

The proportion of variance within groups is equal to $1 - \eta^2(x)$, and equal to the ratio of the within variance and the total variance.

We know from classical regression theory that the 'best' estimate of b for the regression over the total sample, irrespective of group membership, is b_T. It can be shown that the estimate of b_T is a weighted composite of the between-group regression b_B and the within-group regression b_W, as we can see in the following equation:

$$b_T = \eta^2(x)b_B + (1 - \eta^2(x))b_W. \tag{2.7}$$

The first to use equation (2.7) in relation to contextual analysis were Duncan *et al.* (1966). Since then it has been used by, among others, Boyd and Iversen (1979) and Burstein (1980).

A total model does not separate context effects from individual effects. As a result, a total analysis only gives reliable estimates if $b_T = b_W$ and $b_B = 0$ or $\eta^2(x) = 0$, which, again, means there is no context effect. It is clear from equation (2.7) that b_T is only a valid estimate for the individual-level slope if there is no context effect $(\eta^2(x) = 0)$. No context effect means that the relation between x and y is the same within all contexts.

When $b_T = b_B$, it follows that $b_W = 0$ or $\eta^2(x) = 1$. This is the opposite situation to that above, since the effects are exclusively context effects, and individual effects are absent. The relationship between x and y is the same for all individuals, but only if they are in the same context. In most cases where variables are measured at different levels, b_T has a value that is a weighted composite of b_B and b_W, with weights $\eta^2(x)$ and $1 - \eta^2(x)$. If the research is aimed at finding context effects, as in our example of the effect of the sector (public or private) to which a school belongs on the math achievement of their students, the total model is not an appropriate model.

2.5 Total or pooled regression

The first technique we discuss is a simple one. It is not a multilevel analysis, and in most cases not even a contextual analysis. We analyze the effect of homework on math achievement in a single regression for the total sample of ten schools pooled. No school variable is used; the fact that some students are in the same school and others are in a different school is not reflected in the model.

Executing a regression analysis over the total sample of individuals, ignoring group membership, is the same as ignoring the subscript j in equation

Table 2.3 Total regression for 10 schools

	Null model		With homework	
	EST	SE	EST	SE
Intercept	51.3	0.69	44.1	0.98
Slope b_T		n.a.	3.6	0.39
R^2		0.00		0.25
$\hat{\sigma}$		11.1		9.6

root MSE

(2.1). The model becomes

$$y_{ij} = a + bx_{ij} + \varepsilon_{ij},\qquad(2.8)$$

where the ε_{ij} are independent, with mean zero and constant variance σ^2. For completeness, and for later comparisons, we also fit the corresponding *null model*, with only the intercept a and no homework as an explanatory variable. This null model is

$$y_{ij} = a + \varepsilon_{ij}.\qquad(2.9)$$

A regression analyzing individual observations over the total group is called a *total regression*. The individual is the unit of analysis, the unit of sampling and the unit of decision-making. Using this analysis here means that no systematic influence of school on math achievement is expected, and all influences of the school are incorporated in the error term of the model. The fact that the observations are nested within groups is disregarded, and assumed to be of no importance for the research question. In terms of the contextual model (2.2a), in a total regression the intercepts a_j are assumed to be equal for all groups j. The results for the total regression over the ten schools are given in Table 2.3, where we see that one additional hour of study each week will result in an increase in the predicted math score of 3.6 points.

2.6 Aggregate regression

One rather crude way to take the grouping of the students into account is to do a regression over the school means, a so-called *aggregated analysis*. There is a priori no real reason to expect that regression coefficients from a total regression analysis and those from an aggregate regression analysis will be similar. In fact, it is easy to construct examples in which the differences between the two techniques will be very large.

For the analysis we form the 10 homework means $x_{\bullet j}$, the 10 math achievement means $y_{\bullet j}$, and we fit the model,

$$y_{\bullet j} = a + bx_{\bullet j} + \varepsilon_j,\qquad(2.10)$$

where the bullet replaces the index for individuals i to indicate that the x and y are summed over individuals. As usual, it is assumed that ε_j has a mean of zero. The variance of ε_j is now, compared to the total model,

Table 2.4   Aggregate regression for 10 schools

has only an intercept →

weighted by N

	Null model		With homework	
	EST	SE	EST	SE
Intercept	51.3	2.44	37.1	4.03
Slope b_B		n.a.	7.0	1.84
R^2		0.00		0.64
$\hat{\sigma}$		39.3		24.9

$n_j^{-1}\sigma^2$, because it is a mean of n_j disturbances, each with variance σ^2. In this analysis we fit a weighted regression, with weights equal to n_j. The regression is *heteroscedastic*.

Clearly aggregate regression ignores all within-school variation, and thus throws away a large amount of possibly important variance.

The results for the (weighted) aggregate regression are shown in Table 2.4. We see that eliminating within-school variance results in a large increase of the multiple correlation coefficient. At the same time, the standard errors of the regression coefficients become much larger, because they are based on only 10 observations.

Aggregate regression equations must be interpreted carefully. From the prediction point of view, we can merely say that if students in school A spend, on average, one hour more on their homework than students in school B, then A will have an predicted average math achievement score which is seven points higher than B. This does not make any statements about predictions for individual students, and actually making such statements on the basis of aggregated results is known as the *ecological fallacy* (Robinson, 1950).

2.7 The contextual model

The contextual model has been used widely in the past in research interested in the effect of group membership on individual behavior. Typically in this type of analysis the group mean of an individual-level variable is used as a contextual variable. For instance, a characteristic of schools is defined as the average homework time of its students $x_{\bullet j}$ in the next equation, together with the individual student characteristic x_{ij}. The same measurement for homework is used twice in the same regression, once as the original individual measurement, and once as the mean for each school. The mean is 'HomeWork' aggregated from student to school level. The model is thus written as follows:

$$y_{ij} = a_j + bx_{ij} + \varepsilon_{ij}, \tag{2.11a}$$

$$a_j = a + cx_{\bullet j}. \tag{2.11b}$$

Substitution gives us the following equation for the contextual model:

$$y_{ij} = a + bx_{ij} + cx_{\bullet j} + \varepsilon_{ij}. \tag{2.12}$$

Table 2.5   Contextual model for 10 schools

	Null model		With homework	
	EST	SE	EST	SE
Intercept	51.3	0.69	37.1	1.46
Slope b_W		n.a.	2.1	0.43
Contextual effect $b_B - b_W$		n.a.	4.9	0.79
R^2		0.00		0.34
$\hat{\sigma}$		11.1		9.0

The results are presented in Table 2.5. It turns out that the best estimate of b in equation (2.12) is b_W, while the best estimate of c is $b_B - b_W$. For more details, see Duncan *et al.* (1966), Boyd and Iversen (1979) and Burstein (1980), who show that the within regression (b_W) is confounded with the between regression (b_B) in the estimation of the context effect.

Some more technical problems are present in this contextual model, one related to multicollinearity and one to the level of analysis. Multicollinearity is introduced in this analysis by the correlation of the individual variable homework and the group mean for homework. The level of analysis is the individual, because the response variable is defined at the individual level. Performing a regression analysis at one level ignores the true hierarchically nested structure of the data, and treats the aggregated variable as if it was still measured at the student level. The contextual effect in this contextual model is merely the difference between b_B and b_W, or the difference between 7.0, the value of b_B calculated in the aggregated model in the previous section, minus 2.1, the effect of b_W in Table 2.5, which gives us 4.9, the estimated context effect reported in this analysis. It is clear that the individual and group effects are confounded in c, and as a result interesting and significant relationships can be distorted by this procedure.

2.8   The Cronbach model

The Cronbach model (Cronbach and Webb, 1975) provides a clearer picture of the individual effect together with the group mean effect on the response variable. The individual variables are first centered around their respective group means, as in the following equation:

$$\underline{y}_{ij} = a + b_1(x_{ij} - x_{\bullet j}) + b_2(x_{\bullet j} - x_{\bullet \bullet}) + \underline{\varepsilon}_{ij}. \qquad (2.13)$$

In equation (2.13) the centered individual scores $x_{ij} - x_{\bullet j}$ form a variable that is orthogonal to the variable formed by the centered group-level scores $x_{\bullet j} - x_{\bullet \bullet}$. For our 10 schools the centered $x_{ij} - x_{\bullet j}$ scores are the number of hours of homework per week done by each student minus the mean number of hours done in the student's school. Raw scores are thus transformed into deviation scores from the school mean. Centering explanatory variables in this model provides a convenient way of avoiding the problem

Table 2.6   Cronbach model for 10 schools

	Null model		With homework	
	EST	SE	EST	SE
Intercept	51.3	0.69	37.1	1.46
Slope b_W		n.a.	2.1	0.43
Contextual effect b_B		n.a.	7.0	0.67
R^2	0.00		0.34	
$\hat{\sigma}$	11.1		9.0	

of correlation between the two variables that are measurements for 'homework' at the two different levels. The two predictors in the Cronbach model are the centered individual 'HomeWork' and the centered group mean for 'HomeWork' analyzed again with regression. The results are presented in Table 2.6. Because the two predictors are orthogonal, the best estimate of b_1 is equal to b_W, and thus also to the estimate in the contextual model in the previous section. The difference compared to the contextual model is in the estimate for the contextual effect, where b_2 is now equal to b_B and thus equal to the effect of b_B in the aggregate model. Within and between effects are no longer confounded in the Cronbach model.

Although the collinearity problem of the correlation between the individual variable and its aggregated counterpart is solved in the Cronbach model, the significance tests are just as suspect as they are in the contextual model. In both contextual models discussed so far, the analysis is executed at the lower (here student) level. As a result the standard error for the coefficient of the group mean is underestimated. The result is an increase in the alpha level of the test of significance. The group mean has only as many independent observations as the number of groups. Since we have 10 groups with 22 observations each, the total number of observations on which the standard error is based is 220, instead of the correct number, 10. Another threat to the validity of the standard errors in the above contextual model is intra-class correlation. The enhancement of the alpha level when intra-class correlation was present was discussed in Chapter 1. In Section 5.2 we will return to the Cronbach model when we discuss centering of variables around the group mean in multilevel models.

2.9   Analysis of covariance

Analysis of covariance is another traditional way of analyzing our grouped data. Both levels, the school and student level, are included in the model, but not in equal roles. Individual-level explanatory variables are involved, as in regression models, but at the same time schools are allowed to differ in the intercepts. The ANCOVA model incorporates both quantitative and qualitative variables and therefore has a mixed character. It is a regression model, with dummy variables to code group membership. While the regression model enables us to assess the effects of quantitative factors (such as individuals' homework), ANCOVA enables us to model qualitative factors (such as group membership, or the school a student is in).

ANCOVA is a technique with a somewhat different purpose from contextual analyses. It evaluates the effect of groups, correcting for pre-existing differences among these groups. With this technique we can study if schools are equal in achievement, corrected for the differences in the amount of homework done by their students. Such an analysis would tell us if schools differ in average achievement, and which school scores, on average, the best. In ANCOVA the individual effects are neglected, or considered as noise, and the emphasis is on the group (school) effect.

The individual variable(s) functions as covariate(s), while the grouping is used as the important factor in the design. Because the model was originally developed for designed experiments, groups in ANCOVA are considered to be different treatment categories. The equation for the analysis of covariance is

$$\underline{y}_{ij} = a_j + bx_{ij} + \varepsilon_{ij}. \tag{2.14}$$

Different values for a_j mean that some schools have higher 'starting values' for math achievement than others. The assumption in ANCOVA, that all schools have the same slope (the b in the model), means that we assume that the relation between homework and math achievement is the same for all schools.

In the NELS-88 example the results for the ANCOVA are as presented in Table 2.7.

After allowing different schools to start at different levels (different a), the assumption is that one additional hour of homework adds the same increase in math score to a student's score over all schools. We see that equation (2.14) is the same as (2.2a), and that (2.2b) is missing. There is no additional structure imposed on the a_j; they can take all possible values.

Table 2.7 ANCOVA for 10 schools

School	Null model EST	Null model SE	With homework EST	With homework SE
A	45.8	1.77	42.8	1.75
B	42.2	1.90	37.1	2.00
C	53.2	1.73	49.3	1.78
D	43.6	1.81	40.1	1.82
E	49.7	1.81	47.9	1.74
F	46.4	1.90	44.0	1.84
G	62.8	1.03	55.7	1.60
H	49.6	1.85	45.1	1.92
I	46.3	1.85	43.5	1.82
J	47.8	1.90	44.4	1.89
Slope	n.a.		2.1	0.38
R^2	0.44		0.50	
$\hat{\sigma}$	8.5		8.0	

Since ANCOVA expresses the differences between k groups using all $k - 1$ degrees of freedom, this model provides an upper limit on the amount of variance potentially attributable to overall differences in contexts. In contrast to the traditional contextual model in equation (2.1), ANCOVA cannot tell us which characteristics of the context (or school) explain the differences between them. The only thing it shows is how large the overall group effect is, by giving a measure of the explained between-group variation of the intercepts.

The chief advantage of ANCOVA is that it has greater predictive power than the traditional contextual models, as in equations (2.2a) and (2.2b). ANCOVA accounts for all variability between the context means, and not only for variability related to a context-specific explanatory variable, as in contextual models. At the same time the specificity is a strength of the contextual model, because it identifies important group characteristics. Most researchers consider the analysis of (co)variance useful as an estimate of the composite group effect preliminary to contextual analysis. It is true that where the a_j in a covariance analysis adds little explained variance, we know from the outset that none of the context characteristics can explain much additional variance of the response variable in subsequent models. But that is only true if variation among contexts is studied in relation to the intercepts, the main effects. But more and more research is dedicated to studying differences among contexts in relationships between explanatory variables and response variable, the b-coefficients in model (2.14). The assumption of ANCOVA that each of the k explanatory variables, or covariates, has the same relation with the response variable over all schools is unrealistic, as is illustrated in the next chapter. Each school may need its own unique solution, and its own unique relation between the response variable, math score, and the explanatory variable, 'HomeWork'.

2.10   MLn analysis of contextual models

Suppose we have a data file schools.dat with four variables. The first is a student identifier, the second a school identifier, the third the time spent by the student on math homework, and the fourth the math score of the student. There is one record in the file for each student, and the scores of the four variables are separated by spaces.

We start MLn, which will give us an empty worksheet. Into this worksheet we read our four variables, putting them into four data columns:

```
DINPUT C1-C4
```

The program then prompts for a file name, and we tell it to look for schools.dat. This reads the four variables into the four columns. We give them a name:

```
NAME C1   'school'
NAME C2   'student'
NAME C3   'homew'
NAME C4   'math'
```

For the contextual analyses we also need some other variables. These are, respectively, a constant term, the school averages of 'HomeWork' and math, and time and math as deviations from the school average. We first give the columns names:

```
NAME C5   'cons'
NAME C6   'meanhomew'
NAME C7   'meanmath'
NAME C8   'devhomew'
NAME C9   'devmath'
```

and then we fill them, using the appropriate MLn expressions. The first one, PUT, makes a column of ones. The second and third, MLAVE, compute group averages. The last two, CALC, do simple calculations.

```
PUT 260 1 C5
MLAV C1 C3 C6
MLAV C1 C4 C7
CALC C8=C3-C6
CALC C9=C4-C7
```

For the analysis of covariance we also need dummies indicating the schools. We do not bother to give the columns names, we just input

```
DUMMY C1 C10-C19
```

Thus we now have a total of 19 variables, enough to do all the analysis in this chapter.

Let us start with the pooled regression analysis from Section 2.5. We tell the program which variables are explanatory variables, and which is the response variable:

```
EXPL   C3 C5
RESP   C4
IDEN 1 C2
IDEN 2 C1
```

We build the model, indicating which variables we want as fixed effects and which as random effects. By default, all explanatory variables are set as fixed effects. Also cons is the only explanatory variable with a variance component.

```
FPAR C6-C19
SETV 1 C5
```

Once we have switched batch mode on (otherwise the program stops after each iteration), we can start the analysis:

```
BATCH
START
```

2.11 Summary

This chapter discusses some of the traditional ways of analyzing grouped data that consist of two levels, an individual one and a contextual one. The data analysis in these models is always executed at one single level, which can be either the individual or the context level. Analyses executed at the individual level can still be different in the way they handle the between variation. As a result, different regression estimates for the contextual effect are observed among models. From the discussion of the models in this chapter, and the different results, we see that we are in need of a more general model. We need a model that treats the data at the level they are measured, and can answer research questions about the influence of all explanatory variables on the response variable, irrespective of the level in the hierarchy at which they are measured, or to which they are aggregated. Such models are discussed in the next chapter.

Notes

1 In the equations throughout this book, we employ the convention of underlining random variables (Hemelrijk, 1966). This is not entirely standard in statistics, but we think it is very important in comparing the various models with fixed and random coefficients.
2 There is a notational problem here. We have to distinguish the concept of 'mathematics achievement' from the variable or indicator measuring it in NELS-88. If we talk about the concept, we will simply use it in the text without any quotes. The variable or indicator is always in quotes, and is written as one word, such as 'MathAchievement'.
3 We use the symbol $\triangleq$ for definitions.

3 VARYING AND RANDOM COEFFICIENT MODELS

3.1 Introduction

This chapter illustrates the differences between the varying coefficient model approach and its modern version, the random coefficient (RC) approach, using the same sample of 10 schools from the NELS-88 data as used in the previous chapter. But before we do the data analysis the principles behind the two data analysis techniques are illustrated with four hypothetical schools. The illustration shows the differences and the similarities of varying coefficient and random coefficient models. Three hypothetical situations are used for comparison:

- a situation with varying intercepts only;
- a situation with varying slopes only; and
- a situation with varying intercepts and varying slopes.

Varying coefficient models are also known as the 'slopes-as-outcomes' approach.

Using a small sample of four schools, it will be shown that the two models are based on the same concepts, but that the RC model is a statistically more sophisticated version of the varying coefficient model. The concepts are easier to explain using the 'slopes-as-outcomes' approach, while the results of the RC model are easier to interpret. The two models accomplish the same goals and can be used for the same purposes, but the RC model is statistically more correct, more parsimonious, and easier to execute.

After the discussion of the assumptions and formulations of both multilevel models, they are compared with the models discussed in Chapter 2, the traditional regression model and the ANCOVA model. In the last part of the chapter an analysis using the same 10 schools as before shows the differences in data analysis results over the two multilevel models.

3.2 Separate regressions

Traditional strategies for analyzing grouped data are several forms of regression analysis, including ANCOVA. The basic equation defining these linear models is

$$\underline{y}_{ij} = a_j + b_j x_{ij} + \underline{\varepsilon}_{ij}, \tag{3.1}$$

which is similar to equation (2.2a) in Chapter 2.

In equation (3.1) x is again the individual explanatory variable, and y the response variable. The a_j are intercepts and the b_j are slopes. We use the plural form, since instead of the usual single intercept and single slope, separate ones are estimated for each context. To indicate that fact in the formula the subscript j is added to the coefficients a and b. Thus subscript j refers to contexts and subscript i to individuals. The $\underline{\varepsilon}_{ij}$ is the usual individual error term, with an expectation (mean) of zero and a variance of σ^2. In equation (3.1) only $\underline{\varepsilon}_{ij}$ and $\underline{y}_{ij}$ are random variables. Later, when we move away from varying to random coefficient models, the a_j and b_j will be underlined too.[1]

In the 10 schools from our NELS-88 example, students are again the individuals, and schools are the contexts or groups. The explanatory variable x is again 'HomeWork', and the response variable y is 'MathAchievement'.

3.3 Varying coefficients or 'slopes as outcomes'

Within the traditional fixed effects linear framework the 'slopes-as-outcomes' approach can be considered a multilevel analysis approach. This approach is the first step toward modern multilevel modeling. A linear model with individual-level explanatory variables and an individual-level response variable estimates separate parameters within each school, allowing each context to have its own micro model. This is illustrated in the Figures 3.1–3.3 for four hypothetical schools.

The four schools are chosen on the basis of some features they have in common. In Figure 3.1 the four schools have the same slope, but different intercepts. In Figure 3.2 the four schools are chosen because they have the

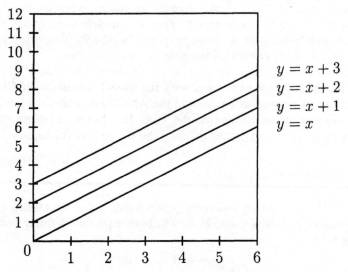

Figure 3.1 Four regression lines, varying in intercept

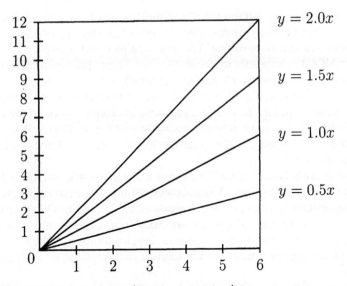

Figure 3.2   Four regression lines, varying in slope

same intercept, but different slopes. The four schools in Figure 3.3 are chosen because the four schools have different intercepts as well as different slopes. In Figures 3.1–3.3 the start of a 'slopes-as-outcomes' analysis is illustrated, where each school has its own regression line. In Figure 3.1 the four schools' regression lines are parallel. Parallel lines mean that the slope of the regression of y, 'MathAchievement', on x, 'HomeWork', is equal for each school. But the lines start at different points, showing that the overall mean level for

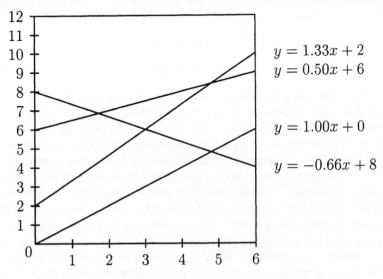

Figure 3.3   Four regression lines, varying in intercept and slope

math achievement is different from school to school. Unequal intercepts mean that some schools perform better, after the amount of homework is taken into account, than others. The situation pictured in Figure 3.1 resembles an ANCOVA solution, where unequal intercepts but equal relationships (or parallel lines) between x and y are assumed.

The four schools in Figure 3.2 are chosen so that all four regression lines start at the same point, thus having the same intercept. But the regression of y on x is stronger in some schools, resulting in different slopes. The steeper the slope, the stronger the relationship between 'HomeWork' and 'MathAchievement'.

The four schools in Figure 3.3 exhibit a more realistic situation for the complete NELS-88 data set. The four schools represent the situation where both intercepts and slopes in the regression model differ. This figure is an example of where the 'slopes-as-outcomes' approach is most valuable. Each school is allowed to have its own unique solution, which may be a more realistic situation than forcing schools to have some or all features in common.

All three figures show that different intercepts and/or slopes are estimated for each context, representing the first step in the 'slopes-as-outcomes' approach. In subsequent steps parameter estimates for intercepts and slopes are used as response variables in macro-level regressions together with macro-level explanatory variables.

Another name sometimes used for this type of analysis is 'two-step analysis', because in a first step the individual, or micro-level, parameters are estimated within each context and used in a second step as response variables, predicted by macro-level variable(s). In both steps ordinary least squares is the estimation method.[2]

The following equations show the second step, which is at the macro level:

$$a_j = c_0 + c_1 z_j, \qquad (3.2a)$$

$$b_j = d_0 + d_1 z_j, \qquad (3.2b)$$

where a_j and b_j are the regression coefficients for intercept and slope respectively. For applications, see Burstein et al. (1978) and Tate (1985).

The number of observations in each step can be different. In the micro analyses of the first step the number of observations varies for each school (see again Table 2.1 in Chapter 2 for our 10 schools). In the macro analyses, with either intercepts or slopes as response variable, the number of observations is equal to the number of schools, which is 10 in our example. Ten schools produce 10 different slopes b_j and 10 different intercepts a_j. The macro equations produce macro intercepts and slopes, which are c_0 and d_0 and c_1 and d_1 respectively in (3.2a) and (3.2b). The same equations show that the group-level variable z is used to explain the variation among intercepts and slopes. For our example z can either be the global variable 'Public', or the aggregated variable 'MeanHomeWork'.[3]

The 'slopes-as-outcomes' approach is promising and a potentially good way to find interesting features in the data, features that were previously ignored. But the approach has a practical disadvantage; it requires a separate analysis for each context. Separate analyses for each school may be the best way to represent each school in its uniqueness, but with a thousand schools (as in the original NELS-88 sample), this method is hardly feasible, not parsimonious, and ignores the fact that schools also have many things in common.

An alternative way is the extension of this approach to RC models, which will be discussed in the next section. This approach combines the conceptually interesting features of the 'slopes-as-outcomes' approach with the statistical advantage of parsimony, and the practical advantage of taking into account not only the uniqueness of each school but also what they have in common.

3.4   The random coefficient model

The RC model is conceptually based on the 'slopes-as-outcomes' model. One difference between the two models is that the RC model does not estimate coefficients for each context separately, although each context is allowed to differ from the other contexts in intercept, in slope(s), or in both. Figures 3.1, 3.2 and 3.3 are compared with similar ones depicting RC models, in order to show similarities and differences between models. Figures 3.1–3.3 showed four separate models estimated for four separate schools, thus providing each school with its own unique solution. The next Figures 3.4–3.6 show the estimation of a single model, from which the four schools are allowed to deviate.

Figures 3.4–3.6 are conceptually equivalent to Figures 3.1–3.3, although not in a visual way. The difference is that in the former only a single solid line is shown, with two dashed lines on either side of it. In each case we have drawn the figure in such a way that the dashed lines capture the variation of the four schools from the average line, corresponding with the variance in the 'fixed but varying coefficient' figures in the previous section. Remember that in Figure 3.1, schools differ only in their intercepts, while in Figures 3.2 and 3.3 schools differ in their slopes as well. The same pattern is followed in the RC figures.

Compare Figure 3.4 with Figure 3.1, where intercepts vary but slopes are all the same. In Figure 3.4 this is reflected in a variance around the line which is regular and equal for all values of x.

Compare again Figure 3.5 with Figure 3.2. Intercepts do not vary, but slopes do. In Figure 3.5 the space around the solid line is not equal for all values of x. This is to be expected in RC models, because variation in slopes is related to values of x, the explanatory variable. The higher the value of x the larger the spread around the mean line in Figure 3.5.

Finally, compare Figure 3.6 with Figure 3.3, where both slopes and intercepts are different for the four schools. As a result the variation around the

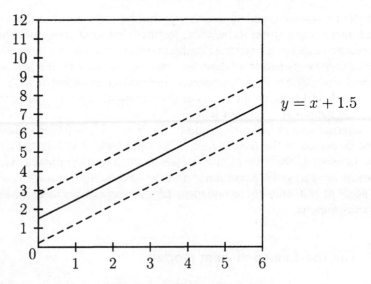

Figure 3.4   Random coefficient solution with random intercept

solid line in Figure 3.6 shows a pattern, produced by the combination of the variance of the slope, the variance of the intercept and the covariance between the two. The variation in slopes is related to values of x, as is the covariance between the variances of intercept and slope. The total variance around the line is the sum of all three (co)variances. As a result, the pattern of the variation of the four schools around the average line is irregular, with a minimum and a maximum at certain values of x.

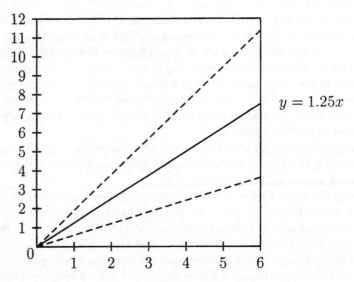

Figure 3.5   Random coefficient solution with random slope

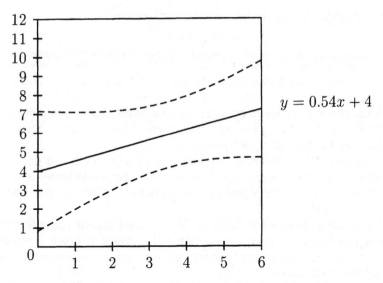

$$y = 0.54x + 4$$

Figure 3.6 Random coefficient solution with random intercept and slope

If the variation around the average line (as indicated by the values for the variances) is large, we say that the single line does not represent all schools equally well. Since the line is an average, we know by the value of the dispersion or variance of the coefficients that some schools are above the line, while others are below it. If, on the other hand, the variances of the intercept and slope are small, the line is close to equal for all schools. A single-level regression analysis would then represent the relationship in this data equally well. Remember that schools can be above or below the line because they differ either in intercept, in slope, or in both. In RC models each coefficient has its own variance, allowing schools to be unique. Uniqueness for each context or school is translated into the extent of the deviation of a school from the overall line. At the end of this chapter it will be explained that this deviation (or error) can be used to calculate the posterior means. Posterior means are separate values for intercepts and slope(s) for separate contexts, very similar to the 'slopes-as-outcomes' approach.

Figures 3.4–3.6 have illustrated the principles of RC modeling , as well as the differences between RC models and 'slopes-as-outcomes' models. Next we formalize the same principles in equation form. The figures show that the coefficient estimates for separate contexts are represented as varying around the overall line. As a result coefficients in RC models consist of two parts: a mean or fixed part, and a variance or random part. The random part is represented by a macro variance, showing the deviation from the overall solution. This variance is referred to as macro-level variance, because the coefficients differ from each other at the macro or context level. The equation of the random model starts with the familiar regression equation, where we underline random variables as before:

$$\underline{y}_{ij} = \underline{a}_j + \underline{b}_j x_{ij} + \underline{\varepsilon}_{ij}. \qquad (3.3)$$

Index i is again used for individuals and index j for groups. $\underline{y}_{ij}$ is the score on the response variable of an observation i within a context j, while x_{ij} is the individual-level explanatory variable of the same observation. The variable $\underline{a}_j$ is the random intercept, $\underline{b}_j$ is the random slope, and $\underline{\varepsilon}_{ij}$ is the disturbance term. We assume that $\underline{\varepsilon}_{ij}$ has expectation zero. All $\underline{\varepsilon}_{ij}$ are independent of each other. The variance of $\underline{\varepsilon}_{ij}$ is equal to σ^2.

Note that the underlining of a and b in equation (3.3) is a new feature, signifying random coefficients. Observe that this underlining is the only difference between this equation and equation (2.2a) for the 'slopes-as-outcomes' model.

The models discussed so far have fixed coefficients. In RC models coefficients can be either fixed or random. The choice between random and fixed coefficients can be made separately for each coefficient in an analysis based on an RC model.

Coefficients in RC models are estimated as a main effect with a variance around it. This variance represents the deviations of contexts from that overall or main effect. To specify the properties of the random coefficients, we define them as fixed components plus disturbances. These disturbances are at the group level. They have expectation zero, as usual, and they are independent of the individual-level disturbances $\underline{\varepsilon}_{ij}$.

The macro-level equations express the properties of the random slope and intercept in terms of overall population values plus error, as specified in the following macro equations:

$$\underline{a}_j = \gamma_{00} + \underline{u}_{0j}, \qquad (3.4a)$$

$$\underline{b}_j = \gamma_{10} + \underline{u}_{1j}. \qquad (3.4b)$$

The macro-level errors $\underline{u}_{0j}$ and $\underline{u}_{1j}$ in (3.4a) and (3.4b) indicate that both the intercept γ_{00} and slope γ_{10} vary over contexts. The grand mean effect in (3.4a) is γ_{00}, while $\underline{u}_{0j}$, the macro-error term, measures the deviation of each context from this overall or grand mean.

In the same manner the grand slope estimate across all contexts is γ_{10}, while $\underline{u}_{1j}$ represents the deviation of the slope within each context from the overall slope, as in equation (3.4b). For the gammas the subscript is defined as follows: the first index is the number of the variable at the micro level, the second represents the number of the variable at the macro level. Hence γ_{st} is the effect of the macro variable t on the regression coefficient of micro variable s. Zero signifies the intercept, that is to say, the variable with all values equal to $+1$, either at the micro level or at the macro level. For instance, γ_{00} is the effect of the macro-level intercept on the micro-level coefficient of the intercept. Note that equations (3.4a) and (3.4b) display the model coefficients $\underline{a}_j$ and $\underline{b}_j$ as a function of two components: a fixed component γ_{00} and γ_{10} respectively, and a random component $\underline{u}_{0j}$ and $\underline{u}_{1j}$ respectively, where $\underline{u}_{0j}$

has variance τ_{00}, $\underline{u}_{1j}$ has variance τ_{11}, while $\underline{u}_{0j}$ and $\underline{u}_{1j}$ have covariance τ_{01}. Table 3.5 summarizes the variance components of an RC model with a random intercept and one random slope.

$$T = \begin{matrix} & \overset{\underline{u}_{0j}}{} \quad \overset{\underline{u}_{1j}}{} \\ \begin{matrix} \underline{u}_{0j} \\ \underline{u}_{1j} \end{matrix} & \begin{pmatrix} \tau_{00} & \tau_{01} \\ \tau_{10} & \tau_{11} \end{pmatrix} \end{matrix} \tag{3.5}$$

The elements in the matrix T in equation (3.5) indicate the extra parameters that are estimated in RC models. The τ parameters show the degree to which the schools differ from the overall line.

To show that the separate equations are not really separate, but part of the model, we substitute the separate equations (3.4a) and (3.4b) into equation (3.3), resulting in

$$\underline{y}_{ij} = (\gamma_{00} + \underline{u}_{0j}) + (\gamma_{10} + \underline{u}_{1j})x_{ij} + \underline{\varepsilon}_{ij}. \tag{3.6}$$

Expanding and rearranging terms yields

$$\underline{y}_{ij} = \gamma_{00} + \gamma_{10}x_{ij} + (\underline{u}_{0j} + \underline{u}_{1j}x_{ij} + \underline{\varepsilon}_{ij}). \tag{3.7}$$

The rearranging of the terms yields an equation that looks a bit more organized. The fixed effects (gammas) are together and the micro error $\underline{\varepsilon}_{ij}$ and the two macro errors $\underline{u}_{0j}$ and $\underline{u}_{1j}x_{ij}$ are also collected together (in parentheses). The result is a single equation that resembles a traditional regression equation, except for the error terms in parentheses. When we discussed Figure 3.6 it was mentioned that the macro-level variance of the slope (the variance of $\underline{u}_{1j}$) was related to the values of x. In equation (3.7), the error term, in parentheses, depends on the variable x.

The uniqueness of each context is expressed in these macro errors (the $\underline{u}$s) which are the deviances from the overall solution. Solutions based on this model no longer produce unique lines for each context, such as the four lines for each of the four schools in the 'slopes-as-outcomes' approach. The result of the RC analysis is a single regression line as an overall solution. Schools fluctuate around this average line. The parameters of the line are the gammas in the above equation, also called the fixed effects. The random effects or macro variances are $\underline{u}_{0j}$ and $\underline{u}_{1j}x_{ij}$. If these variances are significantly different from zero we say that context effects are present.

The equations of the RC model show that this model is an intermediate solution between a totally restricted one, such as a standard regression that ignores the context, and a totally unrestricted one, such as the 'slopes-as-outcomes' approach that takes the context too literally. In the 'slopes-as-outcomes' approach all contexts (or schools in our example), are treated as separate entities as if they have nothing in common, while in the total regression approach schools are treated as if they are the same and interchangeable. The RC model is also statistically in between the two extremes. The RC model estimates fewer fixed parameters than the 'slopes-as-outcomes' approach, but RC models estimate more parameters than are estimated in the total regression model.

In the next section the models discussed in Chapter 2 and in this chapter are compared and summarized.

3.5   Assumptions of linear models

Table 3.1 summarizes the differences between two traditional linear models, regression and ANCOVA, and two multilevel linear models, 'slopes as outcomes' and random coefficients. Most models in Table 3.1 are fixed effects linear models, while the RC model is the only random effects linear model. Within the fixed models the choice is to allow intercepts to be equal (3.8a) or different (3.8b):

$$a_1 = a_2 = \cdots = a_m, \tag{3.8a}$$

$$a_1 \neq a_2 \neq \cdots \neq a_m. \tag{3.8b}$$

Equation (3.8a) applies to the total regression model, where group membership is ignored, and all contexts are assumed to have the same effect on people. ANCOVA models assume unequal intercepts over contexts, as in equation (3.8b) and as shown in Figures 3.1 and 3.4.

Linear models can also differ in what they assume concerning slope coefficients. Slopes can also be assumed to be equal or unequal over contexts. Equal slopes are assumed in the analysis of variance model, where a pooled within slope is estimated, as in equation (3.9a):

$$b_1 = b_2 = \cdots = b_m, \tag{3.9a}$$

$$b_1 \neq b_2 \neq \cdots \neq b_m. \tag{3.9b}$$

Random and varying coefficient models allow slopes to differ, as in equation (3.9b) and as shown in Figures 3.2 and 3.5.

RC and 'slopes-as-outcomes' models allow researchers to assume that coefficients within contexts vary systematically as a function of the context. Different intercepts together with different slopes can be fitted, as shown in Figures 3.3 and 3.6.

ANCOVA and regression are based on a more restrictive model than the two multilevel models. Multilevel models are more general, because some restrictions are lifted and more parameters are estimated. While more general

Table 3.1   Assumptions of traditional linear models and multilevel models

Model	Intercepts	Slopes
Traditional linear regression	equal	equal
ANCOVA	unequal	equal
'Slopes as outcomes'	unequal	unequal
Random coefficients	unequal	either equal or unequal

models allow more freedom than restricted models, they are at the same time less parsimonious. In the next section the RC model and the 'slopes-as-outcomes' model are discussed and illustrated with the same example of 10 schools as used in Chapter 2. Results of the analyses are compared with each other and with the results of ANCOVA.

3.6 'Slopes-as-outcomes' analysis

We now look at an example of the 'slopes-as-outcomes' approach to the analysis of hierarchically nested data. A linear model is fitted within each context, with individual-level explanatory variable(s) and an individual-level response variable. Within-group regression coefficients are used in the next step as response variables in regressions at the macro level. The intercepts and the slopes are model-based aggregates, subsequently used in macro regressions as response variables.

For the analysis of our example with 10 schools, 10 separate regression lines are fitted, one for each school, with 'HomeWork' predicting 'Math-Achievement'. The results are shown in Figure 3.7, where the 10 regression lines are plotted, and in Table 3.2. In the figure the 10 solid lines represent the 10 schools, while the dashed line represents the total regression line calculated over all 10 schools together. Comparing the separate regression

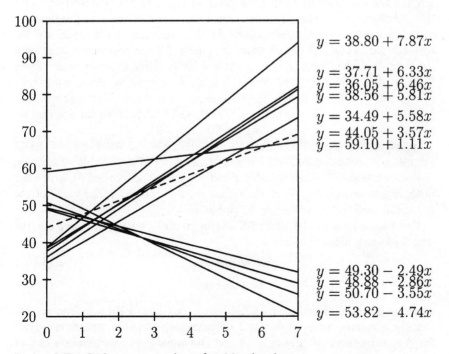

Figure 3.7 OLS regression lines for 10 schools

Separate Regression Table 3.2   OLS regression lines of 'MathAchievement' on 'HomeWork' over 10 schools

School	Intercept Estimate	Intercept SE	Slope Estimate	Slope SE	r	N	Pu/Pr
1	50.70	2.24	−3.55	1.27	−0.52	23	1
2	48.88	3.56	−2.86	1.33	−0.45	20	1
3	38.80	2.94	7.87	1.37	0.77	24	1
4	34.49	1.76	5.58	0.80	0.84	22	1
5	53.82	2.55	−4.74	2.22	−0.43	22	1
6	49.30	1.51	−2.49	1.08	−0.48	20	1
7	59.10	1.42	1.11	0.38	0.34	67	0
8	36.05	3.46	6.46	1.46	0.71	21	1
9	38.56	3.19	5.81	1.99	0.56	21	1
10	37.71	2.36	6.33	1.11	0.80	20	1
Total	44.05	0.98	3.57	0.39	0.50	260	

lines with the overall regression line, we see that schools differ mainly in their slopes and less so in their intercepts from the overall line. The correlation coefficients in Table 3.2 (see the column labeled r) show that the strength of the correlation between 'MathAchievement' and 'HomeWork' varies in a similar fashion to the slope coefficients. This indicates that schools differ substantially in their relationships between 'HomeWork' and 'MathAchievement'. The intercepts differ too, but not so widely. Since we selected the 10 schools for the differences in their relationship between 'HomeWork' and 'MathAchievement', these results are not surprising. The overall regression, calculated over all 260 observations, is also reported in the table; see the row labeled 'Total'. If we compare in Figure 3.7 the regression lines with the overall dashed line, it is clear that schools differ more in their slopes than in their intercepts. The overall line shows a positive slope, while four out of the 10 schools have a negative slope. The main picture shows that schools differ widely in their slopes. For these 10 schools we can see that an overall analysis would not summarize the data well.

In the second step of this analysis the intercepts and the slopes of the 10 schools are used as response variables predicted by the school-level variable 'Public' (with public schools coded 1 and private schools coded 0), which is z in the equations below. Since the public sector is coded 1, the value of the parameter will be the value for the public sector.

The two macro models, one for the intercepts (3.10a), and one for the slopes (3.10b), are:

$$a_j = c_0 + c_1 z_j, \tag{3.10a}$$

$$b_j = d_0 + d_1 z_j. \tag{3.10b}$$

The two macro regressions in equations (3.10a) and (3.10b) produce estimates for a macro intercept (c_0) and a macro slope (d_0), as well as estimates for the main effect of 'Public' (c_1) and the cross-level interaction effect of 'Public' with the slope for 'HomeWork' (d_1).[4]

The results of the macro regressions are as follows:

$$\text{Intercept} \approx 59.10 - 15.95 \times \text{'Public'},$$

$$\text{Slope} \approx 1.11 + 0.94 \times \text{'Public'}.$$

The negative coefficient for 'Public' in the first macro regression with the intercept as the response variable means a lower effect for that sector in general. The positive effect for 'Public' in the second macro regression with the slope of 'HomeWork' as the response variable means a steeper slope for 'HomeWork' in that sector compared to the private sector. The overall effects of the two sectors, after controlling for the amount of homework, can be compared by using equation (3.10a). The effect of the private sector is equal to the macro intercept, which is 59.10, while the same effect of the public sector is lower, $59.10 - 15.95 = 43.15$. The effects of sectors on 'HomeWork' can be compared by using the second macro-level regression (3.10b), which is the regression with the cross-level interaction between slopes and 'Public'. In this regression it shows that the public sector has a stronger effect on 'HomeWork'. The effect is $1.11 + 0.94 = 2.05$, while for the private sector it is equal to the value of the intercept 1.11. In the second step of this analysis 'Public' has two effects, one on the intercept, which we call an overall effect, and one on the slopes, which we call a cross-level interaction effect.

The model of the 'slopes-as-outcomes' approach has some drawbacks. First, the error structure is not specified properly, which makes the p-values for the parameter estimates questionable. Secondly, the regression coefficients obtained in the first step are not equally efficient: some have large standard errors and some have small ones. This is not accounted for in the second step. Each coefficient is weighted equally. The idea of the 'slopes-as-outcomes' approach is, however, appealing. In the next section we show, with the same example, how the idea of the 'slopes-as-outcomes' approach is used in *random coefficient* modeling, but in a more parsimonious way.

3.7 Random coefficient results

The interpretation of the random coefficient model is illustrated, again using the same data with 10 schools, where 'HomeWork' predicts 'MathAchievement'. The software package used for the analysis is MLn (Rasbash *et al.*, 1991).

The solution is (with standard errors below the coefficients)

$$\text{'MathAchievement'} \approx 44.76 + 2.04 \times \text{'HomeWork'}.$$
$$ (2.59) \quad (1.47)$$

Compare the results of the fixed regression model, found in the last row of Table 3.2. This was

$$\text{'MathAchievement'} \approx 44.05 + 3.57 \times \text{'HomeWork'}.$$
$$ (0.98) \quad (0.39)$$

Table 3.3   A random coefficients model

Level 2		
Parameter	Estimate	Standard error
Variance intercept	60.89	29.89
Variance slope 'HomeWork'	19.79	9.53
Covariance slope and intercept	−27.91	15.32

Level 1		
Parameter	Estimate	Standard error
Variance	42.89	3.92
Deviance	1768.21	

As before, 'HomeWork' (x) is positively related to 'MathAchievement' (y), but no longer significantly so. The statement that more hours of homework will result in a higher predicted math achievement score is no longer valid. The differences in the values for the same coefficients over models are minor compared to the much larger differences in the standard errors over models. The coefficient for 'HomeWork', which is significantly different from zero in the fixed model, is no longer significant in the random coefficient model.

Random variation of the regression coefficients is specified in the macro equations (see Table 3.3).[5] To show how the same solution, presented earlier in one single equation, can also be written as two separate equations, we present the same results again:

$$\text{Intercept}_j = 44.76 \times \text{Macro-Intercept} + \text{Error}_j,$$

$$\text{Slope}_j = 2.04 \times \text{Macro-Slope} + \text{Error}_j.$$

The two macro equations can conceptually be compared with the second step in the 'slopes-as-outcomes' approach.

In general, intercepts are more stable estimates than slopes are, resulting in a larger variance of the intercepts than of the slopes. In our handpicked data this is not true. In Table 3.3 both the intercept variance and the slope variance are about equally significant, although not very highly, with calculated standard scores of $z = 2.04$ and $z = 2.08$, respectively. Based on this outcome we conclude that the strength of the relation between 'HomeWork' (x_{ij}) and 'MathAchievement' (y_{ij}) differs across schools roughly as much as the intercepts (the average math scores) do.

3.7.1   Adding a macro-level explanatory variable

We now discuss more ways of employing random coefficient models by further analyzing our small data set. Our next step is to add the second-level variable 'Public' to the analysis model. Sector is used to 'explain' the variation in the coefficients for slope and intercept. By adding a school-level variable z, the variation among schools in general (in the intercepts) or in particular (in the slopes) may disappear. If that works we say that the macro-level variable 'explains' the variation among schools.

The same variables are used at the micro level, that is to say, 'HomeWork' predicts 'MathAchievement'.

As in the 'slopes-as-outcomes' approach, we can choose to model the intercept variance or the slope variance. What we could not do in the 'slopes-as-outcomes' approach was model both variances in the same step. In this subsection we show how the model can be extended by fitting macro variances together. All parameters are estimated in a single model, instead of fitting two different macro models as in the 'slopes-as-outcomes' approach.

Our first task involves the explanation of the intercept variance. For this subsection the macro-level explanatory variable z_j is introduced in the equation of the intercept, but not in the slope. We relate the macro-level variable 'Public' (z_j in the equations) to the intercept by changing the equation in (3.4a) to

$$\underline{a}_j = \gamma_{00} + \gamma_{01} z_j + \underline{u}_{0j}. \tag{3.11}$$

We do not change anything yet in the equation for the slope (3.4b), which remains as before:

$$\underline{b}_j = \gamma_{10} + \underline{u}_{1j}. \tag{3.12}$$

By fitting this model we assume that only intercepts vary as a function of the macro-level explanatory variable z_j plus a random fluctuation, which is represented in the macro-error term $\underline{u}_{0j}$ in (3.11). Note that we actually fit a single model, which becomes clear when we substitute the macro equations (3.11) and (3.12) in the micro equation (3.3). We obtain the single equation

$$\underline{y}_{ij} = \gamma_{00} + \gamma_{01} z_j + \underline{u}_{0j} + x_{ij}(\gamma_{10} + \underline{u}_{1j}) + \underline{\varepsilon}_{ij}. \tag{3.13}$$

Expanding and rearranging terms yields

$$\underline{y}_{ij} = \gamma_{00} + \gamma_{01} z_j + \gamma_{10} x_{ij} + (\underline{u}_{0j} + x_{ij}\underline{u}_{1j} + \underline{\varepsilon}_{ij}). \tag{3.14}$$

Once again, equation (3.14) looks like a fixed effects regression equation with a complex error term.

The results of the analysis for the fixed part are

'MathAchievement' $\approx 57.98 + 1.93 \times$ 'HomeWork' $- 14.57 \times$ 'Public'.
$$\quad\quad\quad (2.67) \quad (1.52) \quad\quad\quad\quad\quad\quad (1.80)$$

The results for the random part are given in Table 3.4. Table 3.4 shows that τ_{00} (the intercept variance) is 'explained' to a certain extent. This is evidenced by the significant (negative) effect of the public sector, and the substantial decrease in intercept variance from 60.89 to 40.20. The fit between the two random coefficient models (with and without 'Public') can be evaluated using the difference between the two deviances of both models.[6] An approximate rule is that a difference in deviance between models should be at least twice as large as the difference in the number of extra parameters estimated.

Table 3.4   A random coefficient model with a
macro variable for the intercept

	Level 2	
Parameter	Estimate	Standard error
Variance intercept	40.20	20.41
Variance slope 'HomeWork'	21.58	10.30
Covariance slope and intercept	−28.95	14.21

	Level 1	
Parameter	Estimate	Standard error
Variance	42.78	3.90
Deviance		1749.48

If the difference in deviance is significant the model with the smallest deviance is considered the 'better' model. If we apply this rule to the models in Table 3.3 and Table 3.4, it appears that the difference in deviance is 18.73 with one degree of freedom. Clearly, the model with 'Public' as a macro variable is more appropriate, since adding this variable improves the fit of the model to the data.

Our next task is to add an explanatory variable that can account for the slope variation among schools. We already know from Table 3.3 that the variance of the slope is significantly random. It is therefore worth investigating if this can be explained by the same macro-level explanatory variable, 'Public'. In notation that means we add z_j to the macro equation (3.4b):

$$\underline{b}_j = \gamma_{10} + \gamma_{11}z_j + \underline{u}_{1j}. \tag{3.15}$$

In this way we have created an interaction of the micro-level variable 'HomeWork' with the macro-level variable 'Public'. Since the private sector is coded 0 the results of the analysis will again show the effect of the public sector only.

Substituting the new macro equation for the slope together with the same macro equation for the intercept as above (3.11), into the basic equation (3.3), we produce the single equation,

$$\underline{y}_{ij} = \gamma_{00} + \gamma_{01}z_j + \gamma_{10}x_{ij} + \gamma_{11}x_{ij}z_j + (\underline{u}_{0j} + x_{ij}\underline{u}_{1j} + \underline{\varepsilon}_{ij}). \tag{3.16}$$

The difference between model (3.16) and model (3.15) is in the estimation of one more parameter. One more coefficient (γ_{11}) is estimated, the rest stays the same.

The results of the fixed part of this analysis are

'MathAchievement' $\approx 59.10 + 1.11 \times$ 'HomeWork' $- 15.83 \times$ 'Public'
                              (6.55)   (4.65)   (6.92)

$- 0.92 \times$ 'HomePublic'
                (4.92)

Table 3.5   Random coefficient model with a
macro variable for the intercept and the slope

Level 2		
Parameter	Estimate	Standard error
Variance intercept	39.84	20.23
Variance slope 'HomeWork'	21.37	10.20
Covariance slope and intercept	−28.68	14.08
Level 1		
Parameter	Estimate	Standard error
Variance	42.78	3.90
Deviance	1749.44	

(handwritten margin note: how do you know whether this is sig. other than the deviance?)

while the random part is in Table 3.5. The results in Table 3.5 show that the cross-level interaction term is not significant. This is also evidenced by the fit of the model compared to the previous one. Comparing the deviances reported in Table 3.4 and Table 3.5 shows that the difference in deviance is only 0.04 with one degree of freedom, not a significant improvement of fit.

The main conclusion of this subsection is that a model with random slope and intercept exhibits a good fit. The macro-level explanatory variable 'Public' shows a negative effect for the public sector on the micro-level intercepts. A cross-level interaction with the same variable and 'HomeWork' does not add significance to the model. The significant random effects can only partly be explained by the school characteristic 'Public'.

It is interesting to compare the solutions obtained in the random coefficient analysis with the solution obtained with 'slopes-as-outcomes' model. The parameters for the intercept and slope are the same among models, respectively 59.10 and 1.11, while the parameter estimates are also very similar, both for the macro-level variable 'Public' (−15.95 versus −15.83) and the interaction term (0.94 versus 0.92). The main difference is in the estimates for the standard errors of the macro-level variable and the interaction.

3.7.2   Posterior means

One type of output that can be obtained from most software for analyzing data with a random coefficient model are posterior means. Conceptually, posterior means are comparable with the coefficients for each school separately, obtained in the first step of the 'slopes-as-outcomes' approach. However, the estimation method for the parameters of a random coefficient model is quite different from the separate OLS estimation in 'slopes as outcomes'. The intercepts and slopes for the 10 schools are estimated in relation to each other as shown before (see again equations (3.11), (3.14) and (3.15)). The estimation method in random coefficient modeling is empirical Bayes maximum likelihood (EB/ML) (the MLn program uses a method which is asymptotically equivalent to EB/ML).

Table 3.6   Shrunken EB/ML regression coefficients
of 'HomeWork' on 'MathAchievement' over 10
schools resulting from a random coefficients model

| School | Intercept | | Slope | | |
	Estimate	(SE)	Estimate	(SE)	N
1	50.28	(−)	−3.14	(−)	23
2	48.77	(−)	−2.70	(−)	20
3	39.24	(−)	7.53	(−)	24
4	35.25	(−)	5.38	(−)	22
5	52.96	(−)	−3.75	(−)	22
6	48.62	(−)	−1.77	(−)	20
7	57.94	(−)	1.35	(−)	67
8	37.16	(−)	6.02	(−)	21
9	39.21	(−)	5.38	(−)	21
10	38.17	(−)	6.09	(−)	20
MLn	44.76	(2.59)	2.04	(1.47)	260

In EB/ML the overall solution is taken into account, where schools with
unreliable estimates are shrunk towards this overall solution. Unreliable
estimates have large standard errors, due to ill-conditioned data and/or
small number of observations within the school. Shrinkage is large when
the estimates are unreliable, and small if the estimates are reliable. Shrinkage
causes the estimates of the posterior means to be different from the estimates
in the 'slopes-as-outcomes' analysis of Table 3.2. Compare the results in this
table with the results in Table 3.6.[7] The posterior means are calculated based
on the overall solution plus the specific OLS solution for that particular
school, and not on separate analyses such as in the 'slopes-as-outcomes'
approach. Standard errors and correlation coefficients within each school
are no longer defined in a straightforward way. They are missing in Table
3.6. The estimates of the overall intercept and slope are again given in the
last row of the table, labeled MLn.

In our example the shrinkage is not large. This is due to the reliability of all
parameters, as can be checked in the separate models solution (see Table 3.2).
All OLS coefficients are significant, because we selected our 10 schools that
way. Still we see the effect of shrinkage for schools with relatively large
standard errors. Compare, for example, schools 5 and 6 in both tables.
Notice also that schools with reliable coefficients, coefficients that are three
or more times as large as the standard errors, remain the same in the analyses
reported in Tables 3.2 and 3.6. In Figure 3.8 the variation among the
posterior means and around the main dashed line is illustrated. The
dashed line represents the values of the gammas or the fixed effects of the
random coefficient analysis. Posterior means are sometimes used to rank
schools, for instance. But the shrinkage factor makes such a use questionable.
Shrinkage means that high-scoring but small schools are shrunk towards the
mean as much as low-scoring small schools are. Both schools may end up
close together in rank. One weakness of the random coefficient model is

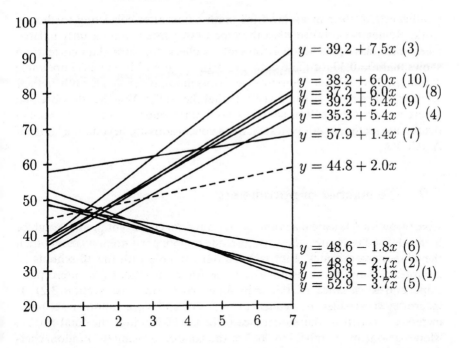

Figure 3.8   Predicted regression lines for 10 schools (shrunken estimates)

that it is less suitable for research that is used for making decisions regarding existing groups, such as schools. The main strengths of the random coefficient model are in exploration of data for development and strengthening of social theories.

3.8   ANCOVA as alternative

For the purpose of explanation we illustrate what the results would have been when using the ANCOVA technique with our small example. We have to realize that executing an analysis of covariance means that you assume that all slopes are equal. We know by now that this is far from true in our data.

In ANCOVA the intercepts are different estimates for each school. Applying ANCOVA to our data produces a regression coefficient for homework on math score, called the pooled within-regression coefficient. The solution for our ten schools is

'MathAchievement' $\approx$ Intercept$_j$ + 3.57 × 'HomeWork'.

The F-test for differences between intercepts gives a highly significant result $F_{9,250} = 13.84, p < 0.0001$. The F-test indicates that some or all schools differ significantly in their mean level for math score, after correcting for home-work. Remember however that the type I error rate is significantly inflated when intra-class correlation is present. A check for intra-class correlation shows that $r = 0.30$ for these data, too high to ignore.[8] It remains impossible within the ANCOVA method to check *why* schools differ significantly in their intercepts. The most we can do is state that they differ. Whether the observed differences are the result of being a school in the public sector or a school in the private sector cannot be tested. Such conclusions are beyond the limits of ANCOVA.

3.9   The number of parameters

Apart from the statistical advantage that random coefficient models produce better-defined estimates, they also provide a more parsimonious model than the 'slopes-as-outcomes' approach. In our example with the 10 schools 30 parameters have to be estimated, three for each school (an intercept, a slope and a variance of the individual error term; see Section 3.2). If macro-level variables are related to intercept and slope, another six para-meters are added to the model (see (3.2a)), which brings the total for the 'slopes-as-outcomes' model to 36. For the same data, using the random coef-ficient model (3.15), the number of parameters is reduced to 8, four variances and four fixed coefficients. The four variances are the micro-level variance, the two macro-level variances, plus their covariance. The four coefficients are the intercept, the micro slope for 'HomeWork', the macro slope for 'Public' and the slope for the cross-level interaction term 'HomePublic'. Simplification of both models makes it possible to estimate even fewer parameters than eight. This can be done by setting the variance of some coef-ficients to zero.

In our example we can set the variance for the slope of the variable 'HomeWork' to zero. If we fit a model with only a random intercept, two fewer parameters are estimated, the variance of the slope and the covariance between the two macro-error variances (for the slope and the intercept). Another solution is that we can keep the variation of the 'HomeWork' slope, since it is significant in the model, but delete the fixed part of the para-meter estimate for 'HomeWork'. This decision can be made based on the individual t-test for both slope parameters, the fixed part and the random part, but a better way is to inspect the overall measure for the fit of the model, the deviances for a model with and a model without the variable 'HomeWork'. Since the differences between the two deviances are chi-square distributed, one model can be tested against another model to see if one is a significant improvement over the other.

Another way of reducing the number of parameters is by eliminating inter-action terms. In our case that would be the model in equation (3.11), which has one parameter less than the model in equation (3.15). In the next chapter we will return to these and other problems while fitting a more realistic random coefficient model to the total sample of 1003 schools. The 10 schools used as an illustrative example in this chapter are just a specific subsample of this larger one.[9]

It is important, in this context, to make a couple of distinctions here. Suppose we use the ANCOVA model, which says

$$\underline{y}_{ij} = a_j + bx_{ij} + \underline{\varepsilon}_{ij}, \qquad (3.17)$$

and again suppose that all groups have the same σ^2. In this model, which has only a single variance component, there are some other 'variances' which are also interesting. The first is the variance of the m numbers a_j, perhaps weighted with group sizes n_j. This is an unknown population quantity. The second is the observed variance of the m numbers $\hat{a}_j$, which are the least-squares estimates from the ANCOVA. We may be tempted to assume that the second (sample) quantity will estimate the first (population) quantity, but the relationship turns out to be more complicated than that.

In the same way, the varying coefficient model,

$$\underline{y}_{ij} = a_j + b_j x_{ij} + \underline{\varepsilon}_{ij}, \qquad (3.18)$$

does not have parameters for the covariance between slopes and intercepts. But we can compute the covariance between estimates of slopes and estimates of the intercepts, and treat this in a way similar to the covariance parameter in random coefficient models.

Thus, although ANCOVA and the other contextual models do not have variance components for the between-group variation, we can define quantities that have a similar function, and we can estimate them from the OLS output.

3.10 Summary

In this chapter we compare two multilevel models, the fixed effect regression 'slopes-as-outcomes' model, and its modern counterpart, the random effects regression model. The first half of the chapter discusses model differences in a theoretical way. Four handpicked schools are used to illustrate possible situations in research and their implications for parameter estimates in both models. The second half of the chapter is an illustration of the results of the 'slopes-as-outcomes' approach and the random coefficient model, using the same data as in the previous chapter, the sample from the NELS-88 data of 10 schools. The results among the fixed and the random model are extensively compared and discussed.

The main conclusion reached in this chapter is that the fixed effect estimates do not differ widely among models, but practical implications of choice of model are quite different. We identified the advantage and the disadvantage of shrinking parameter estimates in the random coefficient model. The advantage is more reliable predictions for the future. The disadvantage is that the estimates are unrealistic for schools that have few observations.

Another practical implication of the difference between models is that the random coefficient model is more parsimonious. Parsimony makes the random coefficient model in many ways desirable, especially when a large number of contexts are present, or if the number of observations within contexts is small. In the last part of the chapter the ANCOVA model is introduced as a means of estimating if context effects in the intercepts are present. ANCOVA is not a serious candidate for the analysis of context effects. All ANCOVA can do is estimate if differences among contexts exists, not why these differences exist.

Notes

1 For simplicity of notation, we only consider models with a single explanatory variable in this chapter, but the extension to multiple regression models is straightforward. In that case we have more than one b in the model, of course.

2 Although the term 'slopes as outcomes' suggests that only slopes are used as response variable in analyses of this type, we emphasize here that intercepts are also used as outcomes. The model should really be called 'intercepts and slopes as outcomes'.

3 Note that second-level error terms are not included in equation (3.2a). Although the specification of the error term is omitted in the equations, this does not mean that it is assumed that intercepts and slopes are measured without error or variation. It only means that this model is statistically not completely identified.

4 Note that the error terms for the macro equations are not present in equations (3.10a) and (3.10b). These macro errors are not defined in the 'slopes-as-outcomes' model. Later we will show that these error terms for the macro regression are defined in the random coefficient model, making the latter model statistically superior.

5 Note that the macro errors are properly defined in the random coefficient model, in contrast to the absence of these macro errors in the 'slopes-as-outcomes' model.

6 A calculated difference in deviance between nested models is chi-square distributed, with degrees of freedom equal to the difference in number of estimated parameters.

7 Note that the parameters in Table 3.6 are based on a single random coefficient model (without macro-level explanatory variables), and calculated in a single step. Standard errors are not provided by the procedure.

8 See again the effect of intra-class correlation on the alpha error in Table 1.1 of Chapter 1. That table shows that an intra-class correlation of 0.20 inflates the assumed alpha level of 0.05 to an observed level of 0.46.

9 Note that the number of parameters in a random coefficient model would not change if we use the total sample of 1003 schools. The number of parameters to be estimated would still be eight. That this is not so when the 'slopes-as-outcomes' approach is used is obvious, since 1003 separate models, with three parameter estimates each, have to be executed in the first step of this approach.

4 ANALYSES

4.1 Introduction

In this chapter we discuss several different analyses based on a sample from the NELS-88 data. We report four modeling sessions, illustrating different ways of using two-level modeling and the MLn package. The estimation method we use throughout is unrestricted maximum likelihood estimation; see Section 5.6.

Each session starts with a small number of variables, picked for theoretical reasons. The selection of a small set of basic explanatory variables[1] is essential for successful multilevel modeling. A more extensive discussion regarding theory-based model choice will be given in Chapter 5, when we discuss the choice between a centered and a raw score model. In this chapter we will show that models can easily become too large. Large and complex models may seem to be more realistic, but only at a price: instability. Instability means that small changes in the model result in large changes in the result of the analysis, due, for instance, to multicollinearity.

An example is the introduction of cross-level interactions. This can best be illustrated by an example. A researcher had three first-level explanatory variables and three group-level explanatory variables. Being most interested in the interaction effects (let us say, between school and student characteristics) the model fitted was:

$$y_{ij} = \beta_{0j} + \beta_{1j}x_{1ij} + \beta_{2j}x_{2ij} + \beta_{3j}x_{3ij} + \varepsilon_{ij}, \tag{4.1a}$$

where the cross-level interactions for the intercept with the three second-level variables z_{1j}, z_{2j} and z_{3j} produce three terms, the so-called main effects of the second-level variables, as in

$$\beta_{0j} = \gamma_{00} + \gamma_{01}z_{1j} + \gamma_{02}z_{2j} + \gamma_{03}z_{3j} + \delta_{0j}, \tag{4.1b}$$

while the cross-level interactions of the three first-level predictors (β_{1j}, β_{2j} and β_{3j}) with the three second-level variables z_{1j}, z_{2j} and z_{3j} produce nine interaction effects, as in

$$\beta_{1j} = \gamma_{10} + \gamma_{11}z_{1j} + \gamma_{12}z_{2j} + \gamma_{13}z_{3j} + \delta_{1j} \tag{4.1c}$$

$$\beta_{2j} = \gamma_{20} + \gamma_{21}z_{1j} + \gamma_{22}z_{2j} + \gamma_{23}z_{3j} + \delta_{2j} \tag{4.1d}$$

$$\beta_{3j} = \gamma_{30} + \gamma_{31}z_{1j} + \gamma_{32}z_{2j} + \gamma_{33}z_{3j} + \delta_{3j}. \tag{4.1e}$$

The nine cross-level interaction terms are in the three separate equations related to the three regression coefficients on the left-hand side of equations

(4.1c) through (4.1e). Reading the separate analysis terms does not show that all these separate terms are calculated in one single step. The estimates of the parameters for main effects in equation (4.1b) and interaction effects in (4.1c) through (4.1e) are all calculated together. Estimates will tend to be correlated; see Section 5.7. Main effects are correlated with interaction effects and interaction effects are correlated among themselves. As a result it is often found that none of the parameters in equations (4.1c) through (4.1e) is statistically significant. If the model is simple, and cross-level interactions are chosen based on theory or knowledge of the data, such zero-effects can very well be a result of multicollinearity. Models like this are not very good for extensive exploration of the data.

The sessions in this chapter show how the data can be explored in different ways, illustrating that many choices can be made. In this chapter the models are used to illustrate the many possibilities of RC models, and the interpretation of the output. The theoretical choice of a model is indicated, but never discussed extensively. Which model is chosen as the 'best' model cannot be decided on the basis of the technique or the model fit. The 'best' model is the model that is best for the given purpose. An example of such a choice is given in Section 5.2, where it is illustrated that using centered scores instead of raw scores has consequences for the results of the analyses. Since different models produce different results, model choice is important. Even the fact that a researcher uses a multilevel model to analyze the data, instead of a traditional regression model, is a choice based on theory and knowledge of the way the data are generated.

4.1.1   Data description

In all four sessions 'MathAchievement' is the response variable.[2] Each sessions starts with a small number of explanatory variables at one or both levels of the hierarchy, the school level and the student level. The general advice in regression analysis to restrict the number of variables in an analysis, especially when they are correlated, is even more pertinent in multilevel modeling. In multilevel models the number of parameters can grow rapidly, as in the example used earlier, where six variables formed nine new interactions, more than doubling the number of explanatory variables in the analysis. Both cross-level interactions and aggregated variables can be added during a session. Other additions to the number of parameters to be estimated are the variances and covariances related to the random slope(s). As in all types of analysis, the most important variables in a multilevel model are chosen based on knowledge of the data and theory. This knowledge and/ or theory will guide the exploration phase, the selection of variables at both levels, the decision as to which coefficients need to be made random, and which cross-level interactions to add to the model.

The analyses reported in this chapter make use of a subsample of seven variables, for 519 students in 23 schools. Eight schools are in the private sector, and 15 schools are in the public sector. This sample is taken from the original NELS-88 data, of 21 580 students in 1003 schools.[3] The smaller sample serves our purposes better, since idiosyncrasies of multilevel modeling show up more readily in small data sets than they do in large ones.

Next to the response variable 'MathAchievement', we selected seven explanatory variables, four student-level explanatory variables and three school-level explanatory variables. The student-level explanatory variables are:

- socio-economic status of parents ('SES');
- the number of hours of homework done per week ('HomeWork');
- the student's race, where white is coded as 1, and non-white coded as 0 (the variable is for that reason called 'White');
- parents' educational level ('ParentEducation').

The school-level variables are:

- education sector, where, as before, the public sector is coded 1 and the private sector is coded 0 (the variable is for that reason called 'Public');
- the percentage of ethnic minority students in the school ('Percent-Minorities');
- class size, measured by the student–teacher ratio ('Ratio').

Aggregated variables are used in some sessions. This adds more school-level variables to the data. These are aggregates from student characteristics to the school level, using the arithmetic mean for that variable in each school.

For obvious reasons we cannot use all seven explanatory variables in one model. If we were to use such a model with all cross-level interactions we would have a model in which the fixed part had 20 fixed parameters. There are coefficients for 'Intercept', 'SES', 'HomeWork', 'White', 'Parent-Education', 'Public', 'PercentMinorities', 'Ratio', 'SES' × 'Public', 'SES' × 'PercentMinorities', 'SES' × 'Ratio', 'HomeWork' × 'Public', 'HomeWork' × 'PercentMinorities', 'HomeWork' × 'Ratio', 'White' × 'Public', 'White' × 'PercentMinorities', 'White' × 'Ratio', 'ParentEducation' × 'Public', 'Parent-Education' × 'PercentMinorities', 'ParentEducation' × 'Ratio'. Needless to say that the cross-level interactions (indicated by 'name' × 'name') are inter-correlated, as well as correlated with the main effects.

The random part of the model becomes equally complicated since all first-level coefficients are random. The random part has 10 parameters, four variances and six covariances. The variances are **V** ('Intercept'), **V** ('SES'), **V** ('HomeWork') and **V** ('White'). The covariances are **C** ('Intercept', 'SES'), **C** ('Intercept', 'HomeWork'), **C** ('Intercept', 'White'), **C** ('SES', 'HomeWork'), **C** ('SES', 'White') and **C** ('Homework', 'White').

Fitting such a large model can easily give misleading results. Correlation among the explanatory variables (including the cross-level interactions) makes parameter estimates in the model unreliable. As a result, slight changes in the model, or the use of a different sample, may lead to different results. In this chapter large models are never used, nor would we recommend the use of such large models in general. We also recommend data exploration

Table 4.1   Correlations among the six explanatory variables
(above diagonal N = 519 and 23 schools, below diagonal
N = 21 580 and 1003 schools)

	'SES'	'HomeWork'	'White'	'Public'	'MeanSES'	'PercentMinorities'	'Ratio'
'SES'		0.30	0.31	−0.55	0.70	−0.05	−0.30
'HomeWork'	0.29		0.09	−0.29	0.33	0.06	−0.16
'White'	0.27	0.08		−0.10	0.24	−0.62	0.08
'Public'	−0.35	−0.12	−0.11		−0.78	−0.04	0.06
'MeanSES'	0.65	0.20	0.28	−0.54		−0.08	−0.42
'PercentMinorities'	−0.23	−0.07	−0.59	0.18	−0.36		−0.22
'Ratio'	−0.12	−0.06	−0.12	−0.12	−0.19	0.12	

before doing a multilevel analyses. The knowledge of the data gained by such an exploration will guide the choice of a small model with only one or two explanatory variables. The variables in the models discussed in this chapter are selected on the basis of theory.

The correlations among the student-level explanatory variables are given in Table 4.1. This shows that even among the main variables correlations are sometimes high – for instance between 'MeanSES' and 'SES' or between 'SES' and 'Public'. In Table 4.1 the values for the correlation in our sample are found above the diagonal, while the correlations for the entire NELS-88 data set are below the diagonal. A comparison shows that especially the correlations among school-level variables ('MeanSES', 'PercentMinorities' and 'Ratio') are different in our sample compared with the correlations in the larger NELS-88 data set. This is not surprising given the larger errors in a sample with 23 schools, compared to the NELS-88 with 1003 schools, and the fact that our sample is handpicked, not randomly sampled. The analyses in this chapter are not used to make generalizations to the NELS-88 sample or to the student population in the USA. The data are a selected sample, used exclusively for illustrative purposes.

In all the model-fitting sessions we make use of MLn statements to indicate a change in a model, to avoid unnecessary use of formulas. The results of the analyses show first the fixed effects (or fixed parameter estimates) in the traditional regression form (with below the coefficients their standard errors in parentheses). A model's variance components, intra-class correlation (when applicable), and deviance are reported in tables, where a clear distinction is made between first-level and second-level parameter estimates.

In the sessions we analyze the data in the way an imaginary researcher would explore the best-fitting model for the data. The choice of explanatory variables in a session is based on theoretical knowledge of the field. The best-fitting model can be determined in a technical sense, by comparing deviances. But alternatively, the best model is determined by the fact that it fits a particular theory. In the modeling sessions we illustrate that after the first choice of what specific explanatory variables to include in the model, many more choices can and have to be made. In all sessions we make our choices explicit.

4.1.2 The organization of the four sessions

The first session with MLn starts by preparing a worksheet that can be saved and used again. For our data we begin by naming all seven variables using the command NAME. In this command the number of the column (C) and the name of each variable are stated, including the identification column for student and school. In our data the school identification code is in the first column, and the student identification code is in the second column. These columns are named respectively school and student, and used to identify the levels of the hierarchy. Level 2 is identified as 'school', and level 1 as 'student' in MLn by using the statement IDEN, as illustrated in the box below.

```
NAME C1 'school' C2 'student'
IDEN 1 'student'
IDEN 2 'school'
```

For model identification we need a response variable and one or more explanatory variables. The intercept is an explanatory variable and it needs to be created in MLn before an analysis can be done. The intercept is a column of ones,[4] hence the name constant (cons) used for this variable in model specification. The constant or intercept is created by coding (CODE) one block of all our 519 observations with a one, as shown in the box below. This column of ones is named cons in the next command. The last command makes the constant an explanatory variable. The constant is made random[5] at the first (SETV 1) and at the second level (SETV 2) by the two last commands in the box below. The constant will be random at both levels in all the models used in this chapter. The variance of the constant at level 1 produces the variance of the familiar first-level error term, while the variance of the second level is the variance of the intercept.

```
CODE 1 519 1 C16
NAMES C16 'cons'
EXPL 'cons'
SETV 1 'cons'
SETV 2 'cons'
```

The variances of the first level can later be used to calculate the multiple correlation within schools. The variance of the intercept at the second level measures the variance of the school-level error terms, and is later used to calculate the multiple correlation between schools.[6] After identifying all explanatory variables, including one or more random slopes, the model can be fitted by starting MLn.

The analysis sessions in this chapter are illustrations of different applications of multilevel modeling. They are organized as follows. In the first session a null model is fitted, followed by a model that answers the simple question: 'Is the number of hours of homework a good explanatory variable for high math test scores?'. The research question can be reworded as: 'What is the relationship between math achievement and a student characteristic, such as the number of hours that is dedicated to homework?'. In the same session parent education, another well-known explanatory variable for school success, is added. Note that the research question does not refer to schools at all. At face value this is not a multilevel research question, and thus we do not seem to need a multilevel analysis. Nevertheless there are good reasons for applying a multilevel analysis in this case.

First of all an intra-class correlation may be present since students are nested within schools, and sampled from within schools. The second reason is the expectation that school effects are present. Effects of schools can be of a general nature and more specific, and both can be fitted in multilevel models. For differences among schools in intercepts an ANCOVA model can be used. But for testing whether slopes differ significantly among schools we need multilevel models. The last conclusion can be reached by either varying coefficient models (see Chapter 3) and/or multilevel models. If differences among schools are present, either in intercepts or slopes, the next question is where these differences come from. Why are schools different? The latter question can never be answered by ANCOVA models since an introduction of school characteristics is not possible in such models. In multilevel models second-level explanatory variables, as well as cross-level interactions, are used for an explanation of variations among schools.

In the second session the analyses of the first session are expanded by adding school-level explanatory variables and cross-level interactions. The variable 'HomeWork' is again the most important student-level explanatory variable for 'MathAchievement'.

In the third session the effects of characteristics of the environment on math achievement are explored. Again the session starts out with no second-level variables, where socio-economic status of the student is used to predict math achievement. Later in the session the school-level explanatory variables 'PercentMinorities' and 'MeanSES' are added.

The fourth and last session mainly discusses cross-level interactions. Interaction effects need large numbers of observations at both levels. This is a possible reason why our subsample did not show significant interaction effects. By repeating the same analyses with the much larger NELS-88 sample (with 1003 schools), it is illustrated that cross-level interactions are present in the data. Cross-level effects need to be strong in order to show up as significant in small data sets. The results with the larger data set also show more stable results, especially for the parameter estimates at the higher level.

4.2   Session 1

4.2.1   Notation for models

Throughout this chapter we will identify models by the commands used in the MLn package. The MLn commands clearly show the differences between one model and the next, without the need to use symbols and equations. Another advantage is that one or two commands may change a model considerably. Our experience with several multilevel modeling software packages has shown that MLn, with its multitude of options, allows users the most control. The downside of that same feature is that researchers need to know the differences between the many options that are offered. As will be illustrated in this chapter, to use MLn (or any other software package for that matter) successfully, one must be clear about what changes to make in models, and what the consequences of these changes are. To indicate what changes are made from one model to the next, the necessary MLn commands are put in boxes.

4.2.2   The null model

This session starts with fitting a null model. A null model contains only a response variable, and no explanatory variables other than an intercept. The null model is used here as a baseline for the estimation of 'explained' versus 'unexplained' variances in comparison to more elaborate models. The null model also provides an initial estimate for the intra-class correlation in the response variable 'MathAchievement'. The variance in a two-level analysis consists of two parts, an individual-level variance and a group-level variance, or a level 1 variance and a level 2 variance. Intra-class correlation is calculated as the intercept variance (a level 2 variance) divided by the total variance (the total variance is the sum of the level 1 and level 2 variances). Another way to express intra-class correlation is as the proportion of the variance that is between groups.

The concept of intra-class correlation is based on a model with a random intercept only. No unique intra-class correlation can be calculated when a random slope is present in the model. The value of the between variance in models with a random slope and a random intercept is a combination of slope and intercept variance (and covariance). We know from the discussion of the basic RC model that the variance of the slope (and, as a consequence, the value of the covariance) is related to the value of the explanatory variable x. Thus the intra-class correlation between individuals will be different, in models with random slopes, for individuals with different x-values. As a result, the intra-class correlation is no longer uniquely defined. The within and between variances of a null model serve as a criterion for estimation of the multiple correlation R^2, a concept known from traditional regression analyses – but again only for random intercept models, not for models with random slopes. A difference between a two-level analysis and traditional regression is that in the latter only one source of variance is present, and thus only one definition of R^2. In two-level analyses two potential sources of variation may be 'explained' by explanatory variables. As a result we have two[7] R^2s. The level 1 R^2 is based on the traditional error variance at the student level, while that of level 2, the school level, is a new concept.

Fitting the null model in MLn needs one more statement, the declaration of cons as an explanatory variable, as shown in the box below. The response variable and the variances for the intercept cons at level 1 and 2 have already been defined (see Section 4.1.2).

EXPL 'cons'

The results of the analysis are

$$\text{'MathAchievement'} \approx 50.76.$$
$$(1.13)$$

The estimate for the intercept (or constant) produces a mean of 50.76, with an estimated standard error of 1.13. The variance estimates, together with the intra-class correlation, are given in Table 4.2. Table 4.2 shows that the within-school variance of math achievement is much larger (81.24) than the between-school variance (24.85). This is a frequently observed result in school effectiveness studies. It indicates that individual students differ more from each other than schools do, or individual variation is larger than school variation. The intra-class correlation, calculated as the ratio of the between variance to the total variance (24.85 divided by 106.09), is 0.23. The deviance reported in the table is equal to minus twice the log-likelihood. This deviance can be used as measure of model fit or improvement of model fit in subsequent models.

The parameter estimates of this null model are used throughout this chapter as a yardstick. For instance, the variances at level 1 and level 2 in the null model can be used to indicate how much reduction in variance takes place in one or both parts, when explanatory variables and/or random slopes are added to models. The deviance serves the same purpose. Differences between deviances in two (nested) models have a chi-square distribution, and this

Table 4.2   Results of model 0

Parameter	Estimate	Standard error
Level 2 variance	24.85	8.60
Level 1 variance	81.24	5.16
Intra-class correlation	0.23	
Deviance	3800.78	

shows, compared to the degrees of freedom lost, if one model is a significant improvement over another. The difference in deviance is especially useful to estimate improvement of fit when the between variance is no longer uniquely defined.[8] For that reason deviances are considered the most important feature in the output, and used for an overall evaluation of models. As a rule of thumb, in order to reach the conclusion that one model is a significant improvement over another, the difference in deviances between two models should be at least twice as large as the difference in the number of estimated parameters.

4.2.3 'HomeWork' and 'MathAchievement'

In this subsection one variable is added to the null model. The model change can be effected by a single statement (see box). The new variable is the number of hours studied at home, 'HomeWork', which is added with a fixed coefficient.[9]

> EXPL 'homew'

The results for the fixed effects are (with standard errors in parentheses)

$$\text{'MathAchievement'} \approx 46.35 + 2.40 \times \text{'HomeWork'}.$$
$$\quad\quad\quad\quad\quad\quad (1.14) \quad (0.28)$$

When these results are compared with the results of the null model we see a change in the value of the intercept. The intercept value was 50.76 before the homework variable was introduced. That the total unexplained variance has also been reduced can be seen when the variance components or random effects are compared over models. The random effects are shown in Table 4.3. First we compare deviances. The difference between the deviance in this table and that in Table 4.2 is 70.29 (3800.78 for the null model minus 3730.49 for the present model). Model 1 has only one extra parameter that needs to be estimated, which is the slope for 'HomeWork'. One parameter estimate is equivalent to the loss of one degree of freedom. A difference in deviance of 70.29, with one degree of freedom, is a significant improvement of fit.

Table 4.3   Results of model 1

Parameter	Estimate	Standard error
Level 2 variance	20.23	7.07
Level 1 variance	71.14	4.52
Intra-class correlation	0.22	
Deviance	3730.49	

Adding 'HomeWork' to the model has reduced the variance at level 1 and at level 2. Calculating the proportion of this reduction results in two measures for 'explained' variance (for more details see Section 5.3), the individual R^2 (denoted R_W^2) and the schools R^2 (denoted R_B^2). The between variance was 24.85 and has fallen to 20.23. The difference of 4.62 is a 19% reduction of the school-level variance. The within variance shows a decrease in variance of 10.10 (81.24 in the null model minus 71.14 in the model in Table 4.3), a 12% reduction. Adding the variable 'HomeWork' results in an R_W^2 of 0.12, and an R_B^2 of 0.19.

4.2.4   Random slope for 'HomeWork'

The next model differs from the previous one in one respect only: the coefficient for the variable 'HomeWork' is allowed to be random. No new variables are added to the model. The reason for fitting this model is the expectation that the effect of 'HomeWork' is different among schools. Differences among schools can be the result of differences in class size, tutoring system or math curriculum. Based on such differences it may be that in some schools students do not need to rely so much on their homework to get good grades in math as in other schools. If indeed the effect of 'HomeWork' on 'MathAchievement' is less strong in some schools than in others we expect to find a significant variance of the slope for 'HomeWork'. One single statement produces this new model (see box below), where the variance for the slope of 'HomeWork' is set at level 2 by the statement SETV 2.

SETV 2 'homew'

The results are

$$\text{'MathAchievement'} \approx 46.32 + 1.99 \times \text{'HomeWork'}.$$
$$\phantom{\text{'MathAchievement'} \approx } {\scriptstyle (1.72)} {\scriptstyle (0.91)}$$

Comparing the results of the random slope model with the previous one shows an increase in standard error for both coefficients, the intercept as well as the slope coefficient. This effect is explained in Section 5.5.

In this model two more parameters are estimated, which are the variance for the slope and the covariance between intercept and slope. These estimates, together with the deviance, are reported in Table 4.4. This shows support for the hypothesis of differences among schools in the relationship between 'HomeWork' and 'MathAchievement'. We base such a conclusion on the significant variance of the slope for homework, which is 16.78 with a standard error of 5.54, giving a z-value of 3.03. Since parameter estimates in regression models can be correlated, interpretations of effects need to be based on the overall fit of the model, more than on the testing of a single parameter in the model. If the fit of the model improves in a significant way, we feel more secure in accepting an individual significant

Table 4.4 Results of model 2

Level 2		
Parameter	Estimate	Standard error
Variance intercept	59.28	20.00
Variance slope	16.78	5.54
Covariance slope and intercept	−26.14	9.65
Level 1		
Parameter	Estimate	Standard error
Variance	53.30	3.46
Deviance	3639.04	

parameter. This way the problem of correlated significance tests is avoided. Since the difference in deviance between model 1 and model 2 is $3730.49 - 3639.04 = 91.45$, with 2 dfr, the model fit is much improved by adding the random slope. The 2 dfr are calculated based on the two extra parameters estimated in model 2. There seems to be support for the conclusion that a model with a random slope for 'HomeWork' is an improvement over a model with a fixed slope.

Adding a random slope means adding two parameters instead of one extra parameter to the model. Intercepts and slopes are negatively correlated, as we see in Table 4.4, where the covariance has a negative sign. Based on the covariance and variances, the correlation can be calculated. The value of this correlation is $r = -0.83$.[10] High correlations between intercept and slope(s) can be avoided by group mean centering the explanatory variables before starting the analysis. How to employ centering is discussed in Section 5.2, together with the resulting changes in the parameter estimates.

In the table three variances instead of one single variance are reported for level 2. In traditional regression a smaller error variance is expected when more parameters are added to a model. In this random slope model we see the opposite. Observe that the intercept variance (level 2) reported in Table 4.2 is 24.85, but is now considerably larger at 59.28, and has a much larger standard error. This is a result of multicollinearity, the high correlation among intercept and slope variances, as indicated by the negative covariance.

An unexpected reduction of the individual or within variance is also observed when model 1 is compared to model 2. The reduction is from 71.14 to 53.30 for model 2. This reduction is unexpected, since only a random part at the second level is added to the model, with no changes at the first level. Reasons for this are given in Section 5.3, where the changes are related to the complexity of the relationship between first-level and second-level variances. Again a way to avoid this is to center the variable 'HomeWork' around the school mean, as explained in Section 5.2, thus removing the between part of this variable, and at the same time the correlation with the second-level parameter estimates. But treating the data in this way results in fitting a conceptually different model, where the variable 'HomeWork' has obtained a specific within-schools part and a between-schools part, which is the mean for 'HomeWork'. In this section we do not deal with this discussion, and continue to use the raw scores for 'HomeWork' and for all other variables added later to the model. The three variances are correlated and cannot simply be summed, while the slope variance is also related to values for x. As a result we no longer have a single value for the between variance and cannot calculate an R^2 between schools. The within variance fluctuates together with the between variance (see Section 5.3), which makes it useless to calculate a reduction in the within variance. Neither could an intra-class correlation be calculated. The familiar concepts of R^2 and intra-class correlation are no longer useful, even in a simple RC model such as model 2.

The conclusion based on the deviance is that adding a random part to the coefficient for 'HomeWork' produces a model with a better fit. But this model is at the same time a more complex model, with the usual disadvantages, such as less stability. In general, it is true that more complex models are also less stable models. In our example this instability shows in the estimate for 'HomeWork'. When compared to the previous model we see the significance drop from a z-score of $2.40/0.28 = 8.6$, showing a highly significant coefficient, to a coefficient that is barely significant with a z-score of $1.99/0.91 = 2.19$.

Users of multilevel models have to be aware that allowing a slope to be random over contexts may result in changes in the coefficients involved. As happens in statistical analyses, there is a trade-off. Here the trade-off is between an improved model fit and a less efficient individual parameter estimate for 'HomeWork'. A choice between the two models cannot be made based on the better model fit, but has to be made based on theory and the purpose of the study. If the effects of schools are the subject of study, then the random slope model is most appropriate. If schools are not the subject of study, a fixed slope may be a better choice. At the end of this section, we will show results of such a traditional analysis.

For the time being, we proceed with this random slope model, since we are interested in school effects. That the coefficient for 'HomeWork' is close to zero is no problem in multilevel analyses, and certainly not a reason for deleting such an explanatory variable from the model. The variable is still a powerful explanatory variable of 'MathAchievement', but in its random effect rather than its main effect. The deviation from this zero value, the slope variance (see Table 4.4) is significant, showing that the effect of 'Home-Work' on 'MathAchievement' is largely an effect of schools, not of individual students.

The next logical step would be to add school characteristics that can explain this variation in the slope of 'HomeWork' among schools, as shown in Session 2. But first we add another student-level variable to the model, which is 'ParentEducation'.

4.2.5 Adding 'ParentEducation'

In this section the theory is tested that math achievement can be enhanced by help offered by parents, where parents with more education are assumed to be most helpful. As a proxy for parental support the explanatory variable 'ParentEducation' is added to our analysis model. Preparation for the analysis is simple. First we locate the variable 'ParentEducation' in the data matrix, and assign the variable the status of an explanatory variable. As shown in the box below, the variable 'ParentEducation' is in column 8 of the data set, and is named pared.

```
NAME C8 'pared'
EXPL 'pared'
```

The model fitted next has two student-level explanatory variables, one with a random slope (homew) and one with a fixed slope (pared). 'ParentEducation' is considered a student-level variable, and not a context variable.[11] The results for the fixed effects estimates of our new model are

$$\text{'MathAchievement'} \approx \underset{(1.76)}{40.81} + \underset{(0.81)}{1.89} \times \text{'HomeWork'}$$

$$+ \underset{(0.29)}{1.85} \times \text{'ParentEducation'}.$$

The results show the expected effect, the coefficient for parental educational level being significant ($z = 6.38$). The estimates of the variance components for this model, together with the deviance, are shown in Table 4.5. The deviance reported in the table has a lower value, indicating that this model exhibits a better fit. This cannot be tested in the usual way, by comparing differences in deviance with the number of degrees of freedom, and using a chi-square test, since the models are not nested. As before, no intra-class correlation and no measure for R_B^2 or R_W^2 can be calculated.

Table 4.5 Results of model 3

Level 2		
Parameter	Estimate	Standard error
Variance intercept	45.20	15.69
Variance slope	13.08	4.41
Covariance slope and intercept	−20.72	7.70
Level 1		
Parameter	Estimate	Standard error
Variance	50.70	3.30
Deviance	3602.35	

For illustrative purposes a model with the same explanatory variables is analyzed using a traditional regression model, and reported in the next subsection.

4.2.6 Traditional regression analysis

Traditional regression analyses ignore the hierarchical structure of data. In our case students are observed within different schools. This means in our data that the substantial intra-class correlation of $r = 0.23$ is neglected, as well as the interaction effect of schools as present in the significant variation in slopes and intercepts among schools. Ignoring intra-class correlation results in general in an underestimation of the standard errors of regression coefficients, suggesting too high precision and resulting in inflated significance levels. See Section 5.4 for some theoretical results. We will show that forcing all schools to fit a single regression where 'HomeWork' predicts 'MathAchievement' results in a loss of important information, as indicated by a less well-fitting model.

In MLn a traditional regression model can be fitted by setting the variance for the constant and the variance for the slope to zero. The statement to clear the variance (CLRV) for the variables cons and 'HomeWork' at level 2 from the previous model is used for that purpose, as is shown in the box below.

CLRV 2 'cons' 'homew'

That this statement changes the model from an RC model into a traditional regression model illustrates again the difference between the two models. The variance components of the regression coefficients of the RC model are removed (cleared) by a single statement, resulting in the familiar regression model with fixed coefficients. The results are

$$\text{`MathAchievement'} \approx \underset{(0.99)}{37.24} + \underset{(0.27)}{2.34} \times \text{`HomeWork'}$$

$$+ \underset{(0.28)}{3.00} \times \text{`ParentEducation'}.$$

The solutions for the fixed effects are different among models. The value of the coefficient for 'HomeWork' in the traditional model is closest to the value of that same coefficient in the multilevel model without a random slope (see Table 4.3); even the value for the standard error is very close to that value. The magnitude of the coefficient of 'ParentEducation' is much higher in the current model. Two out of three standard errors of the regression coefficients are, as predicted, smaller than in the RC model, while the model fit of the traditional model, again as predicted, is lower. The model fit, as indicated by the deviance, is significantly higher for the current than

Table 4.6 Results of model 4

Parameter	Estimate	Standard error
Level 1 variance	75.68	4.70
Deviance	3718.29	

for the previous RC model (see Table 4.6), the difference being 115.94 with an extra 2 dfr.

In traditional regression only one source of error is present, the individual error variance.

A fixed regression analysis can answer questions in relation to students, or, if we aggregate data to the school level, it can answer questions related to schools, but always one level at a time. Multilevel analyses answer both questions at the same time, and are designed to answer questions such as: 'Is the relation between math achievement and homework equal or different among schools, and if so, why?'. As in our examples, we found that adding a random slope for 'HomeWork' to the model resulted in a better fit and a good model for our purposes, which is to test hypotheses related to school effects. We can now proceed by adding school-level explanatory variables to the model, to explore reasons *why* the coefficient for 'HomeWork' is significantly different among schools.

4.3 Session 2

4.3.1 Introduction

In this session we introduce school-level variables. Two useful school characteristics are the size of a school (which we denote 'SchoolSize') and the sector to which it belongs (which, as already explained, we denote 'Public'). Significant variation in intercepts and slopes for 'HomeWork' may be caused by differences among schools. Which characteristics of schools are responsible for these differences is not known. All we can do in this session is to explore if some of the available school-level variables in our data are associated with the observed differences among schools. If variations among schools disappear, either in intercepts, in slopes, or in both, as a result of the adding of these variables to the model, we have indications of *why* schools differ.

Figure 4.1, based on the well-known path model, illustrates the different ways school characteristics can influence lower-level relationships in multi-level analyses. The deviation from the path model illustrates nicely the idiosyncrasies of multilevel models. The diagram can be used to visualize the meaning of the different relationships in the data, without the use of equations. If the reader wishes to make the connection with the equations,

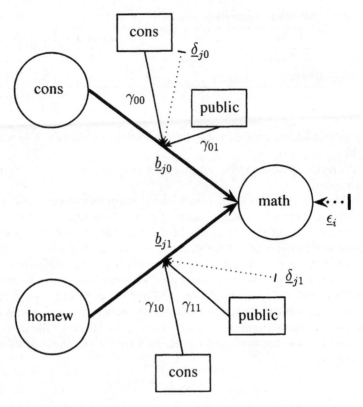

Figure 4.1   Random coefficient regression model

we have provided the symbols for the coefficients next to the path that con-
nects the variables.

In the diagram we illustrate a multilevel model with a single student-level
explanatory variable ('HomeWork'), and a single school-level explanatory
variable ('Public'). The path model has circles and squares, and some
rather unusual paths. The circles represent variables from the student level,
the squares represent variables from the school level. An arrow always
flows from an explanatory to a response variable, but only for the first-
level variables. The paths are interrupted by second-level variables.

School-level characteristics always interact with student-level characteristics, which is indicated by an arrow toward paths instead of towards
variables. This unusual direction of the arrows indicates the difference
between cross-level interactions in multilevel analysis, and direct or indirect
effects as we usually see in path analysis.

In multilevel analyses, when second-level variables are part of the model,
these variables interact with first-level variables, either by having an effect
on the path starting with the intercept, or by having an effect on the path
starting with a first-level explanatory variable. In our example the school-
level variable 'Public' has two cross-level interactions, one with the path

between the constant and 'MathAchievement', and one with the path between 'HomeWork' and 'MathAchievement'.

The gammas in the path model refer to the parameters in the model, and can be compared to the models described in equations in previous chapters. Note that the second-level variable has a constant at the second level, that the two coefficients γ_{00} and γ_{01} replace the one coefficient $\underline{b}_{j0}$ in the path from the constant to 'MathAchievement', and that the two coefficients γ_{10} and γ_{11} replace the one coefficient $\underline{b}_{j1}$. The dotted lines represent the error terms, also known from the equations.

Since 'SchoolSize' and 'Public' are school-level variables, we do not allow these variables to have a random coefficient.[12] The discussion in this chapter is exclusively about random coefficients for student-level variables, where these coefficients vary among schools.

4.3.2 A model with 'SchoolSize'

In the literature on school effectiveness it has been found that smaller schools are more effective in promoting student achievement. Based on this hypothesis a model is fitted with 'SchoolSize' as an explanatory variable at school level. We begin a new session in MLn, where we define the response (RESP) variable 'MathAchievement', and two explanatory (EXPL) variables, 'HomeWork' and 'SchoolSize'. The variance is defined at level 1 and level 2 for the intercept (cons), together with a second variance at level 2, which is the variance for the coefficient of 'HomeWork'.

```
RESP 'math'
EXPL 'homew' 'schsize'
SETV 1 'cons'
SETV 2 'cons' 'homew'
```

The results of this analysis are

$$\text{'MathAchievement'} \approx 44.95 + 1.99 \times \text{'HomeWork'} + 0.43 \times \text{'SchoolSize'}.$$
$$\underset{(2.62)}{\quad} \underset{(0.91)}{\quad} \underset{(0.62)}{\quad}$$

The model fitted has two variables, one student-level variable, 'HomeWork', and one school-level variable, 'SchoolSize'. The results show that 'Home-Work' again has a marginally significant effect. As discussed earlier, the statistically significant fixed effect of 'HomeWork' changed into a borderline effect after the random effect for 'HomeWork' was added to the model, as is the case here. The new variable 'SchoolSize' is not statistically significant when we compare the coefficient with its standard error. Table 4.7 shows the variance components of this model, with their respective standard errors. The deviance of this model is again reported at the bottom of the table. The conclusion that 'SchoolSize' has no effect is supported by the

Table 4.7   Results of model 2

	Level 2	
Parameter	Estimate	Standard error
Variance intercept	62.22	20.90
Variance slope	16.84	5.56
Covariance slope and intercept	−27.27	9.94
	Level 1	
Parameter	Estimate	Standard error
Variance	53.30	3.47
Deviance	3638.61	

lack of improved fit for this model compared to the model in Table 4.4. The present model is similar, except that one more parameter is estimated. This is the coefficient for the variable 'SchoolSize'. Table 4.7 shows that the deviance of our last model is 3638.61, while the model without 'SchoolSize' has a deviance of 3639.04. The difference in deviances is only 0.43, a very tiny improvement. Hence we conclude that for our data 'SchoolSize' has no effect on 'MathAchievement'.

4.3.3   Changing 'SchoolSize' to 'Public'

In this session 'SchoolSize' is deleted from the model and the variable 'Public' is added. In the original data we have a variable 'SchoolSector', which is a categorical variable with five categories (see Appendix), one for the public sector, and four categories for the different private sectors. For our purposes 'SchoolSector' is recoded as a dummy variable, where public schools receive the code 1, while all private schools receive the code 0. An effect found for the variable 'SchoolSector' will be a public school effect, hence the name 'Public' for this variable. We explore whether 'Public' can 'explain' the significant intercept and the slope variances observed in the previous models. In the literature it is reported that the public sector has on average lower student achievement than the private sector has. Based on these findings, a negative effect for the variable 'Public' is expected.

The box below shows a single statement which removes 'SchoolSize' from the model and, at the same time, adds 'Public'.

```
EXPL 'schsize' 'public'
```

The results for the fixed effects are

$$\text{'MathAchievement'} \approx 49.06 + 1.98 \times \text{'HomeWork'} - 4.08 \times \text{'Public'}.$$
$$\quad\quad\quad\quad (2.11) \quad\quad (0.90) \quad\quad\quad\quad\quad (1.90)$$

Table 4.8   Results of model 3

Level 2		
Parameter	Estimate	Standard error
Variance intercept	56.24	19.10
Variance slope	16.37	5.42
Covariance slope and intercept	−25.99	9.44
Level 1		
Parameter	Estimate	Standard error
Variance	53.34	3.47
Deviance	3634.84	

The variable 'Public' has the expected negative sign, and is also statistically significant with a z-score of 2.15. Later we will show that this effect is not very reliable, since the model fit is not greatly enhanced by adding this variable. But given that this effect is a real effect, its negative sign means that a student in the private sector will be predicted to have, on average, a higher math achievement. 'On average' means here that the prediction equation for the private sector has a higher intercept. This intercept is calculated by subtracting the coefficient for 'Public' from the intercept value $(49.06 - 4.08 = 44.98)$. The intercept for the private sector comes out at 4.08 higher than for the public sector. This tells us that on average a student in the private sector has a math score which is 4.08 higher than a student doing the same amount of homework in the public sector. This calculation is of course based on the assumption that the coefficient of 4.08 is a real value, which is a bold conclusion, given the large standard error. The effect of 'Public' may not even be a real effect. This can be checked by comparing the fit of models with and without 'Public'. The deviance reported in Table 4.8, when compared with the deviance in Table 4.4, shows a difference of $3639.04 - 3634.84 = 4.20$. This very small improvement of fit tells us to be cautious in drawing conclusions based on the effect of 'Public'. On the other hand, our model is based on a small data set, with only 23 schools. The power for finding school-level effects when the number of observations is small is very low, unless the effect is very strong. See also Section 5.4.

4.3.4   Adding a cross-level interaction with 'Public'

In the literature we find reports of another kind of public/private school effect, which is that the private sector is found to be more *egalitarian* than the public sector – at least in some respects, as Raudenbush and Bryk (1986) found. They report that the socio-economic status (SES) and minority status of students have less power for predicting student achievement in the private sector than in the public sector, hence producing a less egalitarian effect in the latter sector. Such an effect is called a cross-level interaction in multilevel analysis.

Table 4.9   Cross-level correlation matrix (values for the full NELS-88 data set in parentheses)

	'HomeWork' × 'Public'	'HomeWork' × 'MeanSES'	'HomeWork' × 'Ratio'
'Public'	0.65 (0.52)		
'MeanSES'		0.83 (0.81)	
'Ratio'			0.27 (0.31)
'HomeWork'	0.30 (0.70)	0.43 (0.21)	0.86 (0.89)

Before proceeding to the analysis, a short discussion of interaction effects in regression models, and more specifically in multilevel models, is needed. Adding interactions to regression models in general means adding instability (see Aiken and West, 1991). Interaction terms, such as an interaction between sector and SES (as reported in Raudenbush and Bryk, 1986), are correlated with the original variables, in this example 'SES' and 'Public'. In our next analysis the original variables, 'HomeWork' and 'Public', form the inter-action 'HomePublic'. As a result of this correlation between variables, also known as multicollinearity, we introduce a well-known cause of instability in the model. See Section 5.7 for more discussion of this topic.

In our data 'HomePublic' is correlated with 'HomeWork' ($r = 0.30$) and with 'Public' ($r = 0.65$); see Table 4.9. To show that a high correlation, as found between 'Public' and 'HomeWork', is not an idiosyncrasy of this data set or of these two variables, we show other interactions as well in the same table. The cross-level interactions in Table 4.9 are between 'Home-Work' as the first-level variable and three second-level variables. The second-level variables are 'Public' as discussed before, the mean SES level of each school ('MeanSES') and the class size, as measured by the teacher–student ratio ('Ratio'). All correlations show the same pattern: the cross-level interaction is highly correlated either with the second-level vari-able or with the first-level variable, or with both. The correlations in parenth-eses in the table are the correlations calculated for the large data set, of which our data are a subset. In every case at least one correlation is high. It is safe to conclude that interaction terms introduce instability into the parameter estimates. Centering first-level variables on their respective group means may lower some of the correlations among the variables involved. The effects on the interpretation of centered variables are discussed in Section 5.2.

We proceed with our model by testing a hypothesis that involves a cross-level interaction term. The question is whether the relationship between 'HomeWork' and the response variable 'MathAchievement' is stronger in the public sector than in the private sector. If so, we have found another egalitarian effect of the private sector. A significant negative effect of such an interaction will be interpreted as a private sector effect where the relation-ship is lower than in the public sector. To add the cross-level interaction between 'HomeWork' and 'Public' to the model in MLn means that we need to create it by multiplying (MULT) the two variables involved. The MULT statement in the box below shows that the obtained interaction variable is put in column 19, the first available empty column. A NAME statement for the cross-level variable follows the multiplication statement, by labeling it 'homepub'. To add the interaction term to the model we need an EXPL statement. An interaction term is always fixed in our models, which means that we do not need to make a SETV statement for this new explanatory variable. In the box below the three statements needed for adding a cross-level interaction in MLn are reported.

```
MULT 'homew' 'public' C19
NAME C19 'homepub'
EXPL 'homepub'
```

The result of the analysis is

$$\text{'MathAchievement'} \approx 48.55 + 2.31 \times \text{'HomeWork'}$$
$$\underset{(2.88)}{} \qquad \underset{(1.51)}{}$$

$$- 3.29 \times \text{'Public'} - 0.50 \times \text{'HomePublic'}.$$
$$\underset{(3.55)}{} \qquad \underset{(1.88)}{}$$

The effect of the high correlation among the variables and the interaction is observed in the larger standard error for the coefficient of the variable 'Public', which has nearly doubled. At the same time the effect size for 'Public' is smaller, resulting in a non-significant effect for 'Public'. A similar effect is found for the variable 'HomeWork', where the effect size has increased (from 1.98 to 2.31) but the standard error has almost doubled, with the result that the effect is no longer significant. Since the effect of the cross-level interaction 'HomePublic' is neither significant we would conclude, based on this model alone, that none of the coefficients in the model is significant. A check of model fit compared to the null model can reveal whether this is true. The deviance as well as the variance components of the present model are reported in Table 4.10. The deviance of this model compared to the null model shows that the model fit has improved by 166.01 (compare

Table 4.10   Results of model 4

Level 2		
Parameter	Estimate	Standard error
Variance intercept	56.21	19.09
Variance slope	16.30	5.40
Covariance slope and intercept	−25.92	9.42
Level 1		
Parameter	Estimate	Standard error
Variance	53.34	3.47
Deviance	3634.77	

a deviance of 3800.78 of the null model in Table 4.2 with the deviance in this model of 3634.77). Such a large difference in deviances leads to the opposite conclusion to that based on the individual coefficients for the fixed effects as reported earlier. If we had no prior knowledge of the relations in the data, and did not check with the null model, or the variance components of the present model, we would never conclude that the variables do 'explain' a significant part of the variation in the response variable. This conclusion is based on the deviances and variance components, not on the fixed coefficients. It is still unclear if the introduction of the cross-level interaction variable has introduced instability, hiding significant effects of 'Public', either in the main effect or in the cross-level interaction, or if such effects are not present in the data.

To find significant fixed effects it is best to remove a correlated variable from the model – either the cross-level interaction (which brings us back to model 3) or one of the main effects. The best choice would be based on theory or knowledge of the data. Since we lack such knowledge we decide by comparing model fit. For that purpose we observe the deviances between models with and without some of the variables. In doing so we discover that a model without 'Public' and 'HomePublic', reported in Table 4.4, has a deviance of 3639.04. The difference in deviances between this and our present model of only 4.27 leads us to decide that these models do not differ much from each other in fit. For this data set we give up the hope that one of our hypotheses regarding 'Public' effects can be supported.

Multicollinearity is a problem for the interpretation of the coefficients, especially when dealing with cross-level interactions. Our analyses showed that coefficients for correlated variables change over models, but that their standard errors change even more. The main effect for 'Public' changed from a significant effect of 4.08 (and a standard error of 1.90) to a non-significant effect of 3.29 (and a standard error of 3.55) in a model that contains a cross-level interaction term that is related to 'Public'.

The analyses in this session have not supported the hypothesis that the private sector has a significant effect on student achievement. No such effect seems to be present, either as main effect (an effect on the intercept) or as interaction effect (an effect on the slope). The cause is that either no relationship is present in the data, or the number of observations is too small while effects are weak. Especially in situations where contexts are few or the total number of observations is small, solutions tend to change from model to model as a result of multicollinearity. Stability of solutions can be obtained by using larger data sets with more observations at the individual as well as at the group level. Next we show results with the full NELS-88 data set, containing 21 580 students instead of 519, and 1003 schools instead of 23. We use the same model, where again 'HomeWork', 'Public' and 'HomePublic' predict 'MathAchievement'. The result of this analysis shows highly significant effects for all explanatory variables in the model, contradicting the results obtained earlier.

4.3.5 Analyses with NELS-88

The analyses with the NELS-88 data are based on the last model, model 4. In model 4 the correlations are high between the main effects 'Public', 'HomeWork' and the cross-level interaction 'HomePublic'.

If we repeat model 4, fitting it to a larger data set, the effects are more pronounced. The smaller data set is a subset (although not a random one) of the NELS-88 data. The larger data set is used to show that multicollinearity is less of a problem here than in our smaller data set. The correlations between the variables are again high, as shown in Table 4.9, where it appears that the cross-level interaction is highly correlated with both variables 'Public' and 'HomeWork' (0.52 and 0.70 respectively). The results are

$$\text{'MathAchievement'} \approx \underset{(0.38)}{52.72} + \underset{(0.10)}{0.92} \times \text{'HomeWork'}$$

$$- \underset{(0.43)}{6.05} \times \text{'Public'} - \underset{(0.12)}{0.68} \times \text{'HomePublic'}.$$

Conclusions based on these results are opposite to those based on the same model fitted on our smaller data set. The previous results (in model 4) showed that none of the explanatory variables had a significant effect – neither 'HomeWork', nor 'Public' nor the cross-level interaction 'HomePublic'. The same model fitted to the larger data set shows quite different results, with all coefficients having large effects and small standard errors. Conclusions based on these results are that 'HomeWork' is a significant explanatory variable for 'MathAchievement'. Being in the public sector has a large and significant negative effect on 'MathAchievement', and the cross-level interaction shows a significant negative effect. The negative effect indicates that being in the private sector has a strengthening effect on the relationship between 'HomeWork' and 'MathAchievement'.

Based on the previous model, we concluded that there was no support for our hypothesis about private sector effects. The same analysis repeated here shows that the interaction and the main effect of 'Public' are both statistically significant and negative. These results support both our hypotheses, that there is a private school effect in general and that the private sector is more *egalitarian* in relation to 'HomeWork'. Recall that a positive effect for the private sector (coded as 0) is indicated by a negative sign.

The random effects for this model are shown in Table 4.11. A warning against causal statements regarding the merits of the private versus the public sector is in order here. In general, we know that analysis based on observational data (as opposed to experimental data) is not a strong foundation for making causal statements. The number of intervening variables that could explain the different results of the private versus the public sector is large. In observational data most of the conclusions depend on which variables are present in the model, or which variables the researcher controls before making statements about sector effects. What is interesting in this discussion is that even manipulation of the data, such as centering, can

Table 4.11   Results of model 4 for all of NELS-88

Level 2		
Parameter	Estimate	Standard error
Variance intercept	18.26	1.28
Variance slope	0.44	0.10
Covariance slope and intercept	−0.18	0.28

Level 1		
Parameter	Estimate	Standard error
Variance	71.72	0.72

lead to different conclusions. We will return to this discussion in Section 5.2, where group mean centering of explanatory variables is discussed. The example used in that section is based on the same data and again includes the testing of sector effects. It shows that centering significantly affects our conclusions regarding the sector effect, from negative for the public sector to positive for the public sector. This is again a sign that regression models, random or fixed, need to be interpreted with caution when multi-collinearity is present among variables in the model.

4.3.6   Deleting 'HomePublic' and adding 'White' using the small data set again

The analysis of our small data set did not show promising results for the two school-level variables 'SchoolSize' and 'Public'. Both school characteristics failed to 'explain' the variances of intercept and slope of 'HomeWork' . In the next analyses we redirect our attention to differences in student character-istics. Later we may build a model that includes school characteristics again. The next model tests whether being white (coded as 1) or being non-white (coded as 0) has an influence on math achievement (see the Appendix for the original categories of the variable 'White'). White students are in the majority (75%) in our data.

To go from our previous model to the next model the cross-level inter-action 'HomePublic' is deleted and the student-level variable 'White' is added, as indicated in the box below.

EXPL 'homepub' 'white'

The school-level variable 'Public' and the student-level variable 'HomeWork' are kept in the model. The results of this analysis are

$$\text{'MathAchievement'} \approx 46.61 + 1.91 \times \text{'HomeWork'} + 3.36$$
$$\phantom{\text{'MathAchievement'} \approx 4}_{(2.12)}_{(0.88)}\phantom{1 \times \text{'HomeWork'} + 3.3}_{(0.96)}$$

$$\times \text{'White'} - 3.91 \times \text{'Public'}.$$
$$\phantom{\times \text{'White'} - 3.9}_{(1.72)}$$

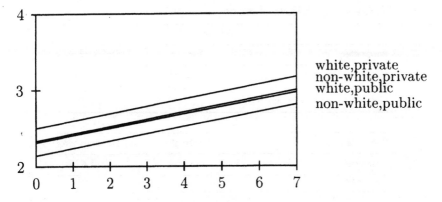

Figure 4.2   Effect of homework by ethnicity and school type

The fixed effects show that being white improves the predicted 'Math-Achievement' by 3.36 points if 'HomeWork' and 'Public' are taken into account. The coefficients of the variables 'White' and 'Public' have opposite signs but are close in magnitude. Based on these two coefficients we could conclude that the predicted math score is lowest for a non-white student in the public sector and highest for a white student in the private sector, given that they both do the same amount of homework. This can be emphasized by plotting four separate lines, as in Figure 4.2. In the figure for each sector two lines are plotted, one for non-whites and one for whites. More so than the magnitude of the coefficients, the figure makes a strong case for the private sector in two ways. It shows an overall private sector effect, since all students score higher in this sector, and it shows an interaction effect, where the non-white students in the private sector do better than both groups in the public sector. But is the conclusion based on this figure reliable? Of course the comparison between the two sectors is not exact, since the coefficient for 'White' has a much smaller standard error, showing that it is a more precisely determined coefficient, than the coefficient for 'Public'. But of greater importance is the possibility of our making a mistake when interpreting the four lines the way we just did.

There are two ways to get an impression of the strength of our findings. One way is to look at the individual coefficients, and the other way is to look at the total model fit. The first information is obtained from the magnitude of the coefficients of 'White' and 'Public' compared to their respective standard errors. It shows a barely significant effect for 'Public' with a z-score of 2.27, and a statistically significant effect for 'White' with a z-score of 3.5. Although statistically significant, the real effect can be close to zero for both coefficients, since the large standard errors show that both are unreliable estimates. The lines in the figure suggest a 'false' sense of certainty. The next way of gauging the strength of the effect of 'White' and 'Public' is to compare the deviances of this model and one that has only 'HomeWork' as an explanatory variable, without the variables 'Public' and 'White'. Such a model can be found in the

Table 4.12   Results of model 5

Level 2		
Parameter	Estimate	Standard error
Variance intercept	52.28	17.88
Variance slope homework	15.83	5.25
Covariance slope and intercept	−25.34	9.08
Level 1		
Parameter	Estimate	Standard error
Variance	52.64	3.42
Deviance	3623.25	

previous section (see Table 4.4). The deviance and variance components of the current model are reported in Table 4.12. The difference in deviance between this model and the model reported in Table 4.4 is 15.79. This improvement is relatively small, given the fact that two more variables are added to the model. It is small enough to warn against overstatement of the effect of the private sector, as is done in the figure.

4.3.7   Adding a random part for 'White'

In the next model a random part is added for the student-level variable 'White'. A single statement is needed for such a change, as shown in the box below. The box shows that the variance for 'White' is set at level 2.

SETV 2 'white'

The results of such a minute change are more extensive than expected. This is true for the fixed effects as well as for the random effects. The fixed effects are

$$\text{'MathAchievement'} \approx 48.18 + 1.95 \times \text{'HomeWork'}$$
$$\underset{(2.26)}{} \quad \underset{(0.88)}{}$$

$$+ \ 2.67 \times \text{'White'} - 4.94 \times \text{'Public'}.$$
$$\underset{(1.50)}{} \qquad \underset{(1.58)}{}$$

This solution shows that the fixed effects for 'HomeWork' and 'Public' are close to the estimates in the previous model. But the coefficient of the variable 'White' has changed considerably, and is no longer statistically significant with a z-score of 1.78. Freeing parameters to be random can introduce instability to a model, which is indicated here by the larger standard error for the fixed part of the coefficient for 'White', which changes from 0.96 in the previous model to 1.50 in the present model.

The same change in significance level of the fixed effect was observed in an earlier section, when the slope for 'HomeWork' changed from fixed to random (compare Tables 4.3 and 4.4).

Table 4.13 Results of model 6

	Level 2	
Parameter	Estimate	Standard error
Variance intercept	64.41	25.86
Variance slope 'HomeWork'	15.68	5.20
Variance slope 'White'	24.22	14.13
Covariance 'HomeWork' and intercept	−26.97	10.41
Covariance 'White' and intercept	−20.27	15.40
Covariance 'HomeWork' and 'White'	2.75	6.31
	Level 1	
Parameter	Estimate	Standard error
Variance	51.15	3.37
Deviance	3618.85	

The price to pay for a random slope seems to be a less stable fixed part of the parameter estimate. The question what to do, whether to make 'White' random or not, is a valid one in this situation. The best way to decide is based on theory. For instance, we may reason that math achievement is not an individual student effect (being white or non-white), but a school characteristic. In the light of that theory our present model fits reality better than the previous model did. In any case, it is clear that the two last models, seemingly the same, show different results in the fixed effects. That the changes in the random part are also large is clear from the variance components in Table 4.13.

Addition of a single random slope has added three more variances to the model, one variance for the slope of 'HomeWork', and two covariances between the latter variance and the variance of the constant and the variance of 'HomeWork'. The variance for the coefficient of 'White' is not significant with its value of 24.22 and a standard error of 14.13, resulting in a z-score of 1.71. It seems that there is no support for the hypothesis of school characteristics causing the differences in white versus non-white students in math achievement.

But again we have to be careful with this interpretation. Multicollinearity again comes into play. When the variance components in Table 4.13 are compared to the ones in Table 4.12, some unexpected changes are observed. One of these is the decrease in the within-variance component, from 52.64 to 51.15, as a result of the addition of a second-level variance component. This is unexpected, since the error terms at different levels are assumed to be uncorrelated (for more details on variances and their inter-relationships, see Section 5.3). Larger changes are observed in the intercept variance, which increased from 52.28 to 64.41, while its standard error increased as well. This change can be explained by the correlations among the variances, as indicated by the covariances. Altogether it tells us that estimates can no longer be interpreted at face value.

A more technical approach to deciding if the random slope is a worthwhile addition to the model is to look at the goodness of fit. The deviance of the present model (see Table 4.13) is 3618.85, an improvement of 4.40 with three degrees of freedom lost. Adding a random slope has not had the expected result of an improvement of fit.

In the first session in this chapter we found that a model with a random slope for 'HomeWork' improved the fit of the model considerably. The same cannot be said for the random slope of 'White'. If we have a theory to guide us, a decision could be made to delete either the random slope for 'HomeWork' or the random slope for 'White'. Since we have no such theory we base our decisions on the goodness of fit, and set the variance for the coefficient of 'White' to zero again.

Note, however, that we do not claim that the decision to make the slope for 'White' fixed again is the correct one. If other variables entered the equation, or if some are deleted, the slope for 'White' could be found to be significantly random.

4.3.8   Making the coefficient of 'White' fixed and adding 'MeanSES'

In the next multilevel analysis an aggregated school-level variable 'MeanSES' is created. The student-level variable 'SES' is aggregated to school level by calculating its mean for each school. In MLn the statement MLAV creates this mean, as is shown in the box below. This aggregated variable is put in the first available column in our data set, which is C20, under the name 'meanses'.

```
MLAV 'school' 'ses' C20
NAME C20 'meanses'
```

The effect of 'MeanSES' is first explored. If 'MeanSES' has a significant influence it should lower the significant between-school variance in intercepts. Later the same variable is used to 'explain' the other significant variation in the model, which is the variance of the coefficient for 'HomeWork'. In the box below the MLn statements are reported that clear the variance at level 2 for the variable 'White' and add 'MeanSES' to the model.

```
CLRV 2 'white'
EXPL 'meanses'
```

Before the results of the analyses are reported we need to point out a source of multicollinearity in the data. There is a high correlation between

Table 4.14   Results of model 7

Level 2		
Parameter	Estimate	Standard error
Variance intercept	50.11	17.20
Variance slope 'HomeWork'	15.43	5.10
Covariance slope and intercept	−25.50	8.92
Level 1		
Parameter	Estimate	Standard error
Variance	52.72	3.43
Deviance	3616.83	

the two school characteristics 'Public' and the average SES level of a school. In our small data set this correlation is $r = -0.78$, while for the full NELS-88 data set the correlation is $r = -0.54$ (see Table 4.1). The negative sign of this correlation indicates that students in public schools have, on average, lower SES than students in private schools. This correlation affects the estimated values for these coefficients, as the results of the analysis show. The value of the coefficient for 'Public' falls close to zero, and is no longer significant. The coefficient for 'MeanSES' is, however, significant with a z-score of 2.76, as will be seen from our new model:

$$\text{'MathAchievement'} \approx \underset{(2.14)}{44.58} + \underset{(0.87)}{1.93} \times \text{'HomeWork'} + \underset{(0.95)}{3.14} \times \text{'White'}$$

$$+ \underset{(2.12)}{0.17} \times \text{'Public'} + \underset{(1.82)}{5.03} \times \text{'MeanSES'}.$$

The important question is whether the difference is due to 'Public' or 'MeanSES'. Again this should be decided based on some theory. Such a theory, for instance, discusses the influence of 'SES' on math achievement. We can also proceed with observing deviances. Based on goodness of fit, we can decide what 'explains' more, the variable 'Public' or the variable 'MeanSES'. The deviance of the current model is reported in Table 4.14, together with the variance components. The model shows a slight improvement over model 5, the model without 'MeanSES', with a difference in deviances of $3623.25 - 3616.83 = 6.42$.

4.3.9   Deleting the school characteristic 'Public'

Based on the knowledge that 'SES' has an influence on students' achievement, let us keep 'MeanSES' and delete 'Public'. The deviance of a model with only 'MeanSES' as a school-level characteristic can be compared with that of a model with only 'Public' as a school characteristic. A difference in deviance will give us a measure of goodness of fit of one model compared to the other.

To set up this new model one command is needed, which is the toggle command EXPL. This deletes 'Public' from the model, as shown in the box below.

$$\boxed{\text{EXPL 'public'}}$$

The results for the fixed effects are

$$\text{'MathAchievement'} \approx \underset{(1.74)}{44.68} + \underset{(0.87)}{1.93} \times \text{'HomeWork'}$$

$$+ \underset{(0.95)}{3.15} \times \text{'White'} + \underset{(1.28)}{4.93} \times \text{'MeanSES'}.$$

It will be evident that the standard error for the coefficient of 'MeanSES' is now lower than in the previous model. This is the direct result of removing the correlated variable 'Public'. The prediction here is that being white in the school with the highest 'SES' will result in the best math results, given the same number of hours of homework.

The random effects and the deviance of this model are given in Table 4.15. The deviance shows that the deletion of the variable 'Public' does not worsen the model fit. The deviance reported in Table 4.15 is 3616.83, equal to that in the previous model (see Table 4.14), indicating that deleting the variable 'Public' does not change the fit of the model. Comparing the deviances of models 5 (see Table 4.12) and 8 (see Table 4.15) shows that the model with the school-level variable 'MeanSES' fits better than the model with 'Public'; compare the deviances of the two models, respectively 3623.25 and 3616.83. Based on the better fit of a model with 'MeanSES', we decide to continue our exploration of the data with this model. Again we want to stress that this decision, based on goodness of fit, is not an optimal decision. The best decision is made on theoretical grounds. In this case we also happen to believe on theoretical grounds that 'MeanSES' is a better predictor of math achievement than 'Public'. We proceed with a model that contains 'MeanSES' and add a cross-level interaction with that variable and the student variable 'HomeWork'. A cross-level interaction means here that

Table 4.15   Results of model 8

Level 2		
Parameter	Estimate	Standard error
Variance intercept	50.01	17.20
Variance slope 'HomeWork'	15.42	5.10
Covariance slope and intercept	−25.49	8.92
Level 1		
Parameter	Estimate	Standard error
Variance	52.72	3.43
Deviance	3616.83	

'MeanSES' is used to 'explain' the significant variance in the slope of 'HomeWork'.

4.3.10   Adding an interaction between 'HomeWork' and 'MeanSES'

In previous analyses we concluded that the slope for 'HomeWork' is significantly random, but were unable to 'explain' th: variation among schools. Neither 'SchoolSize' nor 'Public' showed a significant interaction with 'HomeWork'. In this session the aggrega ed school-level variable 'MeanSES' is used with the same purpose: to 'explain' the variation in schools in the slope for 'HomeWork'. First we need to create a cross-level interaction. This is done in MLn, as before, by using the calculation statement CALC, as shown in the box below. (In Section 4.3.4 the interaction term was constructed by using the multiplication statement MULT. Both ways will produce the desired effect.) The new variable is named 'HomeSES' and added to the model with the EXPL statement.

```
CALC C21 = 'homework' * 'meanses'
NAME C21 'homeses'
EXPL 'homeses'
```

The results for the fixed effects of this model are

$$\text{'MathAchievement'} \approx \underset{(1.76)}{44.58} + \underset{(0.88)}{1.99} \times \text{'HomeWork'} + \underset{(0.95)}{3.15} \times \text{'White'}$$

$$+ \underset{(2.88)}{3.99} \times \text{'MeanSES'} + \underset{(1.56)}{0.57} \times \text{'HomeSES'}.$$

These results are disappointing. The cross-level effect is non-significant and the model fit has not improved. In fact the model is at face value a worse model, since the standard error of the variable 'MeanSES' has changed from 1.28 to 2.88, while the magnitude of the coefficient has dropped. The main effect for 'MeanSES', which was previously a significant effect with a z-score of 3.88, has become a non-significant effect with a z-score of 1.40. If this model were our only analysis, we would conclude that 'MeanSES' has no effect, neither as a main effect or as a cross-level effect. This would be an incorrect conclusion given what we know from the previous analysis. The same conclusion is reached here as in model 4. The high correlation between the main effect 'MeanSES' and the interaction effect 'HomeSES' ($r = 0.83$; see Table 4.9) has made the model unstable.

In Table 4.16 the deviance and variances are reported. By comparing the deviance with the deviance reported in Table 4.15, it appears that adding the cross-level interaction has not improved the model fit. The difference in deviance between the two models is 0.13. The price paid for the addition of the interaction term is an increased instability of the individual coefficient

Table 4.16   Results of model 9

| Level 2 | | |
Parameter	Estimate	Standard error
Variance intercept	49.90	17.13
Variance slope homework	15.28	5.06
Covariance slope and intercept	−25.32	8.86

| Level 1 | | |
Parameter	Estimate	Standard error
Variance	52.73	3.43
Deviance	3616.70	

for 'MeanSES', as indicated by the larger standard error. This shows again that adding correlated variables to a model, in this example the addition of cross-level interactions, increases instability in parameter estimates. Multicollinearity affects models fitted to small data sets more than it affects large data sets, as we have already shown.

4.3.11   Adding another student-level variable

In the literature on school effectiveness SES plays an important role. It is well documented that higher-SES students score on average higher on achievement tests than low-SES students. The same is observed for schools, where high-SES schools have, on average, higher-scoring students than low-SES schools. In the previous analyses we fitted models with 'MeanSES'. In this analysis we add the individual 'SES' variable as a student-level explanatory variable to the model.

Our new model has three student-level explanatory variables, 'Home-Work', 'White' and 'SES', with one school-level explanatory variable, 'Public', and no cross-level interactions. To fit this new model in MLn, the variable 'SES' is added and the interaction term 'HomeSES' deleted by means of a single EXPL statement, as shown in the box below.

```
EXPL 'homeses' 'ses'
```

The results for the fixed effects are

$$\text{'MathAchievement'} \approx \underset{(1.71)}{45.65} + \underset{(0.83)}{1.83} \times \text{'HomeWork'} + \underset{(0.96)}{2.22} \times \text{'White'}$$

$$+ \underset{(0.53)}{2.21} \times \text{'SES'} + \underset{(1.37)}{2.97} \times \text{'MeanSES'}.$$

All variables have z-scores of around 2.00, except for the student variable 'SES', which has a z-score of 4.17. As expected, adding the student-level variable 'SES' to the model lowers the estimate for the school-level variable

Table 4.17   Results of model 10

	Level 2	
Parameter	Estimate	Standard error
Variance intercept	46.60	16.10
Variance slope 'HomeWork'	13.78	4.60
Covariance slope and intercept	−23.02	8.16

	Level 1	
Parameter	Estimate	Standard error
Variance	51.12	3.32
Deviance	3600.08	

'MeanSES' ($r = 0.70$; see Table 4.1). Comparing parameter estimates shows a change in the magnitude of the coefficient for 'MeanSES' from 4.93 in model 8 to 2.97 in the model above. The standard error changed from 1.28 in model 8 to 1.37 in the model above.

The deviance is reported in Table 4.17. As before, the deviance is used to check if adding the variable 'SES' improves the overall model fit. Comparing the deviances of this model and that in Table 4.15 shows a difference of 16.75 with one degree of freedom lost. The same table shows that the within as well as the between variances are slightly lower as a result of the addition of the variable 'SES'.

Models fitted to larger data sets suffer less from unstable results when multicollinearity is present among the explanatory variables in the model. Another advantage of large data sets is that they are more powerful in detecting cross-level interaction effects. We illustrate this again by repeating the last model with the full NELS-88 data set.

4.3.12   Analyses with NELS-88

The model repeated with NELS-88 is the previous one, model 10. This model has three explanatory variables – 'HomeWork', 'SES' and 'MeanSES' – that are highly correlated (for the correlations, see Table 4.1). The variables 'SES' and 'MeanSES' in particular have a high correlation, $r = 0.65$.

The results of model 10 with the large data set are

$$\text{'MathAchievement'} \approx \underset{(0.17)}{47.61} + \underset{(0.05)}{1.22} \times \text{'HomeWork'} + \underset{(0.15)}{1.78} \times \text{'White'} + \underset{(0.09)}{3.73}$$

$$\times \text{'SES'} + \underset{(0.21)}{4.00} \times \text{'MeanSES'}.$$

The results for the fixed effects are very different from the effects of the previous model. There are several reasons. First, our previous analysis was based on a small data set, which is not a random sample from the large NELS-88 data, but selected for a specific purpose. For that reason the

Table 4.18　Results of model 10 for all of NELS–88

	Level 2	
Parameter	Estimate	Standard error
Variance intercept	7.39	0.74
Variance slope 'HomeWork'	0.35	0.08
Covariance slope and intercept	−0.79	0.22
	Level 1	
Parameter	Estimate	Standard error
Variance	66.12	0.66

magnitude may have changed. Secondly, the standard errors are much smaller, which is a direct result of the larger number of observations at both levels in the NELS-88 data. The very small standard errors have changed the significance level for all coefficients. The z-score for 'HomeWork' is 24.4, whereas it was 2.20 in the model fitted to the smaller data set. The same is observed for the coefficients of 'White' with a z-score of 11.87 (previously 2.31), for 'SES' with a z-score of 41.4 (previously 4.17), and for the coefficient of the school characteristic 'MeanSES', with a z-score of 19.05 (previously 2.17). Thus the barely significant coefficients for the reduced data set become very significant when the larger data set is used.

The random effects are reported in Table 4.18.

4.4　Session 3

4.4.1　'SES' as a student-level explanatory variable

In this session hypotheses are tested relating math achievement to the environment of the student. Environment is defined at two levels, the individual home environment, and the school environment. Individual environment is measured by the socio-economic status (SES) of the parents, which is a composite of their educational level and income. As proxies for the school environment, percent of minorities in a school and the mean SES are used.

We begin a new session in MLn, defining the response (RESP) variable 'MathAchievement', the explanatory (EXPL) variables 'cons' (for the intercept or constant) and 'SES', plus the variance at level 1 and level 2 for the intercept.

```
RESP 'math'
EXPL 'cons' 'ses'
SETV 1 'cons'
SETV 2 'cons'
```

Table 4.19 Results of model 1

Parameter	Estimate	Standard error
Level 2 variance	11.80	4.61
Level 1 variance	75.20	4.77
Intra-class correlation	0.22	
Deviance	3748.36	

The statements in the box indicate that we start with the single explanatory variable 'SES' at the student level. The random coefficient for the intercept is the only variation at the student and at the school level. The results of fitting this model are

$$\text{'MathAchievement'} \approx \underset{(0.83)}{51.20} + \underset{(0.56)}{4.35} \times \text{'SES'}.$$

The results show that the fixed coefficient for 'SES' has a highly significant effect, with a z-score of 7.77. This individual effect of 'SES' can only be taken seriously if the total model fit is improved. Model fit is again measured by a comparison of the deviance of this model with the deviance of this model without the explanatory variable 'SES', which is the null model fitted in Session 1.

The deviance, together with the random effects of this model, is reported in Table 4.19. Comparing the deviance of this model with the null model (with a deviance of 3800.78; see Table 4.2), shows a difference of 52.42. The difference is large enough to support the earlier finding that the student's home environment has an effect on math achievement.

The variance components have also changed, as compared to the null model. The between variance of the intercept has fallen from 24.85 in the null model to 11.80, a reduction of 53%. By our definition of 'explained' variance we can say that R_B^2 is 0.53. The within variance has also fallen, from 81.24 in the null model to 75.20 in our new model, a reduction of 7%. It could be said that R_W^2 is 0.07. Based on this analysis, we find that the effect of 'SES' is largely a between-schools effect. The larger between-schools component of the variable 'SES' raises the expectation that the coefficient of 'SES' may be significantly random among schools.

For a further discussion of the within and between R^2 in multilevel models, as well as the limited usefulness of such concepts, we refer to Section 5.3.

4.4.2 Adding a random slope

In the next analysis we add a random slope to the model, based on the argument that a different relationship between 'SES' and 'MathAchievement' may exist among schools, for instance as a result of different teaching styles. An egalitarian teaching style, such as mastery learning, sets as a goal that all students reach the same results, irrespective of their background. Other teaching styles are more meritocratic, where pre-existing differences in students are enhanced, perhaps by ability grouping. Differences in teaching styles may lead to different relations between 'SES' and 'MathAchievement'.

To add a random slope for 'SES' to our previous model we need a single MLn command, which sets the variance of the slope for 'SES' random at level 2 as is shown in the box below.

SETV 2 'ses'

The results for the fixed effects are very similar to the previous model:

$$\text{'MathAchievement'} \approx \underset{(0.83)}{51.20} + \underset{(0.56)}{4.35} \times \text{'SES'}.$$

From previous analyses we know that adding a random part to a coefficient can change the magnitude of the fixed effect, and may change the standard error of that coefficient as well. This effect of the addition of a random slope was observed in two previous analyses, one in Session 1, where the explanatory variable was 'HomeWork', and one in Session 2, where the affected variable was 'White'. In both cases the addition of a random part to the model changed a highly significant effect into an effect close to zero. But in this analysis nothing changed.

A look at Table 4.20, which contains the variance components and deviance, shows the reason why the fixed effect for 'SES' is not affected by adding a random part. Remember that adding a random slope adds two more parameters estimates to the model, one for the variance of the slope and one for the covariance between this slope and the random intercept. The most obvious feature in the table in the variance components at level 2 is the zero variance for the slope of 'SES', as well as for the covariance. Everything in this table is equal to the previous model, where no random slope was present, the variance of the intercept is the same, as are the level 1 variance and the deviance. It is clear that this model is equal to the previous model, since no random slope for 'SES' is estimated. Setting variances that do not converge to zero is the result of the way MLn is programmed. If

Table 4.20   Results of model 2

Level 2		
Parameter	Estimate	Standard error
Variance intercept	11.80	4.61
Variance slope	0	*
Covariance slope and intercept	0	*
Level 1		
Parameter	Estimate	Standard error
Variance	75.20	4.77
Deviance	3748.36	

variances become close to zero the iteration process is slowed down. The solution in MLn is to set to zero variances that are close to zero, in order to speed up the process. Other software may take different decisions in such cases, and produce non-significant variances after an endless number of iterations. An unusual number of iterations is in all cases a sign that a model does not fit the data very well.

The hypothesis that some schools are different from others in their relationship between 'SES' and 'MathAchievement' is not supported by the data.

4.4.3 Adding 'PercentMinorities'

Our model is expanded by adding a school characteristic, which is 'PercentMinorities'. The slope for 'SES' is changed from random to fixed, by a statement that clears this variance at level 2 (CLRV). The two MLn commands necessary for fitting this new model are in the box below.

```
CLRV 2 'ses'
EXPL 'minority'
```

The results of the analysis are

$$\text{'MathAchievement'} \approx \underset{(1.13)}{53.12} + \underset{(0.56)}{4.34} \times \text{'SES'} - \underset{(0.35)}{0.80} \times \text{'PercentMinorities'}.$$

'SES' has a coefficient that is very similar to the estimates in previous models, with much the same magnitude and standard error. It is very clearly statistically significant, with a z-score of 7.75. The coefficient of 'PercentMinorities', with a z-score of 2.29, is significant. Comparing deviances among models also reveals minor changes in model fit as a result of the addition of 'PercentMinorities'. The deviance and the random components of our analysis are reported in Table 4.21. The effect of 'PercentMinorities' is present in the variance component of the second level. Variances can be affected at one or both levels by addition of variables to the model. For instance, both variances may become smaller when a first-level variable is

Table 4.21   Results of model 3

	Level 2	
Parameter	Estimate	Standard error
Variance intercept	9.43	3.90
	Level 1	
Parameter	Estimate	Standard error
Variance	75.02	4.76
Deviance	3743.39	

added to the model. The expectation is that a student-level variable will have a large within component, and as a result reduces the within variance the most.

In the analyses presented so far the student-level variables 'SES' (used in this session), and 'HomeWork' (used in the first session) both have larger between component as indicated by the larger reduction of the between variance. Addition of a school-level variable affects the between variance only, since it has by definition only a between-schools effect, and a zero within effect. The expectation is that the between variance (of the intercept) is smaller in our current model as a result of adding 'PercentMinorities' as compared to a model without 'PercentMinorities'. As predicted, the intercept variance of 11.80 in Table 4.19 is reduced to 9.43, a reduction of 2.37, or an increase of 9.5% in the 'explained variance' of the between part. Forcing student-level variables to affect the within variance only, can be done by way of school mean centering. That centering explanatory variables in this way has consequences for the interpretation of analyses results is discussed in Section 5.2. The trade-off here is that centering has technical advantages (see also Section 5.3), by splitting within and between variances into two distinct parts.

The deviance of this model (see Table 4.21) is 4.97 smaller than the deviance of the model without 'PercentMinorities' (see Table 4.19) where the deviance is reported to be 3748.36. This small improvement and the increase in R_B^2 are reasons for keeping 'PercentMinorities' in the model.

The within variances of level 1 are not compared over models. We assume that adding a second-level variable will not change the within variance. In multilevel models the within and between disturbances are uncorrelated. Second-level variables only have a between component, unlike first-level variables, which have a within and a between part. In the next analysis 'MeanSES' is added as another proxy for school environment. We will demonstrate that model fit, increase in R^2, and individual parameter estimates show contradictory results, and we will indicate that the total model fit is the best way to measure the improvement of a model, as well as the reliability of the individual parameter estimates.

4.4.4 Adding 'MeanSES'

Our next model is an extension of the previous model, with a second proxy for school environment, 'MeanSES'.

```
EXPL 'meanses'
```

This variable is almost not correlated with the school-level variable 'Percent-Minorities' in the reduced data set, with $r = -0.08$ (see Table 4.1). A higher correlation is evident in the full NELS-88 data set. This negative correlation

Table 4.22 Results of model 4

	Level 2	
Parameter	Estimate	Standard error
Variance intercept	7.23	3.23
	Level 1	
Parameter	Estimate	Standard error
Variance	75.08	4.76
Deviance	3739.61	

of $r = -0.36$ indicates that the higher the percentage of minorities in a school, the lower the socio-economic status of that school tends to be. The results of the analysis with both school characteristics are

$$\text{'MathAchievement'} \approx \underset{(1.03)}{53.08} + \underset{(0.61)}{3.89} \times \text{'SES'} - \underset{(0.32)}{0.68} \times \text{'PercentMinorities'}$$

$$+ \underset{(1.39)}{2.86} \times \text{'MeanSES'}.$$

In this model the individual coefficient for 'MeanSES' is barely significant, with a z-score of 2.06, while the coefficient for 'PercentMinorities' stays very much the same, again significant with a z-score of 2.13. It will be interesting to see if the model fit has improved. The deviance, used for this procedure, is reported in Table 4.22. Checking the deviance of the model in Table 4.22 and comparing it with the deviance in Table 4.21 or Table 4.19 shows the same result. The improvement in deviance of the current model compared to the first model (the model without 'PercentMinorities' and 'MeanSES'), is slight, with a difference of 8.75. Comparing the last two models with each other, the difference in deviance is 3.78, showing that the addition of 'MeanSES' has hardly changed the goodness of fit.

It is also interesting to observe that the between variance, the variance of the intercept, is lower as a result of the adding of two school-level variables. In terms of 'explained' variance, the two variables 'explain' 18% which may lead a researcher to the conclusion that these two variables do contribute fairly strongly to our model. For instance, the between variance was 11.80 in Table 4.19, became lower in Table 4.21, where we concluded that the addition of 'PercentMinorities' 'explained' 9% of the between variance, while Table 4.22 shows again a lower between variance of 7.23, again a 9% increase in R_B^2. Calculating the total R^2 within and between, using the null model, we observe that the between variance has been reduced from 24.85 in the null model to 7.23 in the current model, a reduction of 17.62, and comparable to an R_B^2 of 0.71. The variable 'SES' 'explains' 53% of the between R^2, while 18% is 'explained' by the two school characteristics. The within variance falls from 81.24 in the null model to 75.08 in our last model, a difference of 6.16. This reduction is comparable to an R_W^2 of 0.08.

We want to emphasize here that the individual parameter estimate for 'MeanSES' and the increase in 'explained' variance contradict the conclusion based on the model fit. When in doubt, researchers should use model fit as the criterion. The fit of the total model is a more reliable measure than individual parameter estimates and/or increased R^2.

To illustrate once again that larger numbers of observation make a difference, the second and third analyses are repeated with the full NELS-88 data set. This will show that:

- the variance for the slope of 'SES' is no longer set to zero, although the interpretation of this coefficient does not change;
- that the coefficients for 'PercentMinorities' is highly significant instead of barely significant as in the analyses above; and
- the deviance of a model without 'PercentMinorities' is much smaller than the deviance of a model with 'PercentMinorities'.

4.4.5   Analyses with NELS-88, models 2 and 3

The first analysis is a model with 'SES' as an explanatory variable, and a random instead of a fixed coefficient, which is a repetition of model 2. The model is repeated with a more powerful data set to reproduce the reported significant difference among schools in the relationship between 'SES' and 'MathAchievement' (see Raudenbush and Bryk, 1986). Our previous failure to replicate these results may be due to the low power of our small sample for finding school effects. Remember that the number of schools in our small sample is only 23, while there are 1003 schools in the full NELS-88 data set, making it much more powerful (for more details on power, see Section 5.4).

Our expectation is that the earlier reported zero estimates for the variance of the slope for 'SES' and its covariance with the intercept will change to a non-zero and significant effect in this analysis. The results of a model with a random slope fitted to the NELS-88 data are

$$\text{'MathAchievement'} \approx 50.96 + 4.82 \times \text{'SES'}.$$
$$\underset{(0.12)}{} \quad \underset{(0.10)}{}$$

Smaller standard errors for all coefficients in the analysis are observed, due to the larger number of observations. But that is not what we want to explore. We want to check if the slope of 'SES' is significantly different among schools. The results are given in Table 4.23, where the variance components are reported. Based on the magnitude of the variance component for the slope compared to its standard error in Table 4.23, we conclude that the slope is again not significantly random. This time the output of MLn reports values for both variances, but the results are the same. The slope variance is 0.54 with a standard error of 0.35. The hypothesis that the relationship between 'SES' and 'MathAchievement' is different among schools is again not supported by the data.

Table 4.23 Results of model 2b

Level 2		
Parameter	Estimate	Standard error
Variance intercept	11.11	0.66
Variance slope	0.54	0.35
Covariance slope and intercept	1.68	0.33

Level 1		
Parameter	Estimate	Standard error
Variance	69.76	0.70
Deviance	154 336	

For illustrative purposes we also reanalyze model 3 with our larger data set. We add the school-level variable 'PercentMinorities' and set the variance for the slope of 'SES' to zero, as illustrated in the box below.

```
CLRV 2 'ses'
EXPL 'minority'
```

The results are

$$\text{'MathAchievement'} \approx \underset{(0.19)}{53.16} + \underset{(0.09)}{4.76} \times \text{'SES'} - \underset{(0.05)}{0.71} \times \text{'PercentMinorities'}.$$

Comparing the results reported in Table 4.21 with the fixed effects of the same model 3 fitted to the smaller data set reveals smaller standard errors for the full NELS-88 data set. The barely significant coefficient for the school-level variable 'PercentMinorities' ($z = 2.29$ in the earlier model) has become very significant ($z = 14.2$ in last model). The model we fitted has a random intercept only, and the variances of the intercept at level 1 and level 2 are given in Table 4.24. The variance components show the same feature as the fixed effects, which is smaller standard errors. Comparing the deviance of 154 184 with the earlier model, fitted to the same data, shows that the deviance in Table 4.24 is much smaller, with a difference of 152.

Table 4.24 Results of model 3b

Level 2		
Parameter	Estimate	Standard error
Variance intercept	8.78	0.55

Level 1		
Parameter	Estimate	Standard error
Variance	69.93	0.69
Deviance	154 184	

Calculating R^2, as before, shows comparable effects of the variables on the between and within variance. For that purpose we need to fit first a new null model, with no explanatory variables. This null model shows a within variance of 76.62, and a between variance of 26.56. Comparing the between variance in Table 4.24 with the null-model between variance shows a reduction of 17.78, which amounts to a between R^2 of 0.67. Comparing the within variance of our last model with the potential within variance of the null model shows a reduction in within variance of 6.69, showing a within R^2 of 0.09. Although the small data set is not a random sample of the NELS-88 data, the effects of the same model on the within and between variance are very similar. The two variables 'SES' and 'PercentMinorities' together 'explain' a large part of the between variance, while the variable 'SES' explains a small part of the within variance.

Our exploration of the influence of environment, as defined at student level by 'SES' and at school level by 'PercentMinorities' and 'MeanSES', has shown some effects of the environment on math achievement. The one thing that is still puzzling is the non-significant variance for the coefficient of 'SES'. We return to the topic of a random or non-random slope for 'SES' in Section 5.2. For the discussion here, the effect of centering on the random part of the slope for 'SES' is of interest. It will be illustrated in Section 5.2 that centering around the school mean changes the slope for 'SES' so that it becomes very significantly random over schools – an observation not made when a raw score model is used, as illustrated above.

4.5   Session 4

4.5.1   Analysis with class size and a cross-level interaction

In our analyses of the small data set we have not yet found a significant cross-level interaction. Since we have more school-level explanatory variables in the data set let us try again, this time by using class size as measured by the teacher–student ratio; this variable is called 'Ratio'. A higher 'Ratio' means a larger class size. Class size is an important determinant of student achievement given the latest school reforms in California, where millions of dollars have been spent on reducing class sizes in an attempt to improve the low standing of California's public school system. If smaller classes predict higher achievement, we expect the sign of the coefficient for 'Ratio' to be negative in our data analyses.

This effect of class size is measured in two different ways: first as an overall effect, and secondly as an interactive effect. The interaction effect will be between 'Ratio' and 'HomeWork'. This interaction is added as a test of the hypothesis that students need to do less homework when class sizes are small. Under this hypothesis we expect a positive interaction effect, where the strength of the relationship between 'HomeWork' and 'MathAchievement' will be stronger when classes are larger.

Table 4.25   Results of model 1

	Level 2	
Parameter	Estimate	Standard error
Variance intercept	59.30	20.01
Variance slope 'HomeWork'	16.80	5.55
Covariance slope and intercept	−26.25	9.67
	Level 1	
Parameter	Estimate	Standard error
Variance	53.30	3.47
Deviance	3638.82	

To prepare the model for the new session in MLn we start again by defining all the variables that are needed. The response (RESP) variable is 'Math-Achievement', the explanatory (EXPL) variables are 'cons' (for the intercept or constant), 'HomeWork' and 'Ratio'. For the variance part we define the variance at level 1 and level 2 for the intercept, and at level 2 for 'HomeWork'.

```
RESP 'math'
EXPL 'cons' 'homew' 'ratio'
SETV 1 'cons'
SETV 2 'cons' 'homew'
```

The results of the analysis are

$$\text{`MathAchievement'} \approx 47.97 + 1.99 \times \text{`HomeWork'} - 0.10 \times \text{`Ratio'},$$
$$\phantom{\text{`MathAchievement'} \approx }{\scriptstyle(3.92)}\phantom{+ }{\scriptstyle(0.91)}\phantom{\times \text{`HomeWork'} - }{\scriptstyle(0.20)}$$

which do not support our hypothesis, since the individual coefficient for 'Ratio' is not significant. However, interpreting individual parameter estimates can be misleading when explanatory variables are correlated. The correlation between the two explanatory variables is not large because $r = -0.16$ in this data set. Just to make sure we are correct in concluding that there is no main effect for 'Ratio', the deviance of the current model is compared with a model with only 'HomeWork'(see Table 4.4), where the deviance is 3639.04. The deviance of our current model is reported in Table 4.25, with a value of 3638.82. This deviance show a decrease which is too small to contradict the earlier finding. The conclusion is that 'Ratio' has no effect on math achievement for our small data set.

4.5.2   Interaction between 'Ratio' and 'HomeWork'

After this lack of success we test a second hypothesis, also related to 'Ratio'. This hypothesis states that in smaller classes the relationship between math achievement and number of hours of homework will be less strong. As a result, we expect that students who need to do a lot of homework benefit the most from smaller classes. In statistical terms we state that 'Ratio' has an interaction effect. If the hypothesis is supported we expect to find a significant cross-level interaction effect between 'Ratio' and 'HomeWork'.

We create this cross-level interaction in MLn by multiplying (MULT) the two variables with each other and put the new variable in the first available empty column of our data set, which is C22 in this case. Next we name this variable 'HomRatio', as shown in the box below. With the familiar command EXPL the new variable is added to the model, while 'Ratio' is deleted in the same command. Note that the assignment of the newly created interaction term to C22 is arbitrary. The rule is to assign a new variable to an empty column, which in this case was 22.

```
MULT 'homew' 'ratio' C22
NAME C22 'homratio'
EXPL 'ratio' 'homratio'
```

The results of this analysis are

$$\text{'MathAchievement'} \approx 46.32 + 2.91 \times \text{'HomeWork'} - 0.05 \times \text{'HomRatio'}.$$
$$\quad\quad\quad\quad\quad (1.72) \quad (2.06) \quad\quad\quad\quad\quad\quad (0.11)$$

Again the results do not support the hypothesis of an interaction effect of 'Ratio', since this parameter is not significant. The same is observed when the deviance is compared with the deviance of a model with only 'Home-Work', as we did before. We found that the deviance of such a model was 3639.04 (see Table 4.4), while the deviance of our present model is 3638.79 as reported in Table 4.26, showing again a negligible improvement of fit. When comparing the fixed effect estimates over the last two models it appears again that introducing a cross-level interaction introduces instability, as a result of the correlations among the variables. The correlations between the two variables in the current model, 'HomeWork' and 'HomRatio', can be found in Table 4.9, where the interaction term has a correlation of $r = 0.86$ with 'HomeWork'. As a result of this high correlation the (barely)

Table 4.26   Results of model 2

Level 2		
Parameter	Estimate	Standard error
Variance intercept	59.35	20.03
Variance slope 'HomeWork'	16.79	5.55
Covariance slope and intercept	−26.27	9.68
Level 1		
Parameter	Estimate	Standard error
Variance	53.3	3.47
Deviance	3638.79	

significant slope for homework in model 1, with an estimate of 1.99 and a standard error of 0.91, is no longer significant in model 2, with a higher estimate of 2.91, but also a higher standard error of 2.06.

Again a different conclusion is reached when the same model is analyzed with the larger NELS-88 data set. Cross-level interactions are more easily detected when the number of observations (within as well as between) is larger than 23 schools and 519 students. (For more on power, see Section 5.4.)

4.5.3 Repeating the modeling session with NELS-88

Using the complete NELS-88 data set, three models are fitted with the explanatory variables 'HomeWork', 'Ratio' and 'HomRatio'. In all three models 'HomeWork' is included, with a random coefficient. The results are reported together in Table 4.27 for easy comparison. The top half of the table shows the fixed effects, while the bottom half shows the random effects. The first model in the table includes all three variables. The second model contains only a main effect for 'Ratio' and is the same as model 1 with the small data set in this session. The third model has the interaction term, but not the main effect of 'Ratio', as in model 2 with the small data set in this session. The results in Table 4.27 show that the high correlation between 'HomeWork' and 'HomRatio' ($r = 0.89$) affects the estimate for 'HomeWork' in the same way as in the small data set. If the interaction term is part of the model (see the new model and model 2 in Table 4.27) the standard error of the coefficient for 'HomeWork' is much larger. The magnitude of the coefficient for 'HomeWork' is also larger in model 2, which may be the result of the deletion of the variable 'Ratio', which has correlation $r = -0.06$ with 'HomeWork' (see Table 4.1) and $r = 0.31$ with

Table 4.27 Analysis with 'Ratio' and cross-level interaction on full NELS-88 data set

PARAMETER	New model		Model 1		Model 2	
	EST	SE	EST	SE	EST	SE
Cons	51.43	0.70	51.52	0.61	47.90	0.19
Homew	1.52	0.18	1.48	0.05	2.00	0.16
Ratio	−0.20	0.04	−0.21	0.03		
Homratio	−0.003	0.01			−0.03	0.008
Level 2						
Cons/cons	23.29	1.51	23.28	1.51	24.19	1.55
Homew/cons	−0.91	0.31	−0.91	0.31	−1.06	0.32
Homew/homew	0.52	0.10	0.52	0.10	0.54	0.10
Level 1						
Cons/cons	71.74	0.72	71.74	0.72	71.74	0.72
Deviance	155679		155679		155706	

'HomRatio' (see Table 4.9). The cross-level interaction term has a significant coefficient in model 2, where the main effect for 'Ratio' is deleted. Comparing deviances (see last row in Table 4.27) shows that the two first models fit the data equally well, indicating that the cross-level interaction does not add to the fit of the model. For reasons of fit we can opt to delete the interaction variable, and keep the main effect of 'Ratio' in the model – but only if we have strong beliefs that this interaction is not important in a theoretical sense, as compared to the main effect.

Summarizing the differences in results between the large data set and the small data set, we see that the coefficient for the interaction term is significant when introduced without the main effect of 'Ratio'. Secondly, we find a strong effect for 'Ratio' with a z-score of respectively 5.00 in the new model and 7.00 in model 1 of Table 4.27.

4.6   Discussion

The analyses in this chapter illustrate one important fact. Do not bother to do any hypothesis testing for individual regression coefficients, look at the model fit. In the life of the real (rather than virtual) scientist, hypothesis testing is almost never useful. Usually researchers are interested in exploring to see what the data tell them. They want some notion of how fuzzy the situation is, based on the data only, or, in certain desirable but rare situations, wish to understand what conclusions can be drawn from the data based on both their prior understanding and the current data. Neither of these situations is handled by hypothesis testing.

To illustrate, we can compare the analysis of the 23 schools with the same analysis over 1003 schools in the large NELS-88 data set in Section 4.5.3. It is hard to defend any conclusions based on a hypothesis test (a z- or t-test) of a single parameter estimate when using a small data set. We have discovered that some models show no single parameter to be significant in the small data set, but the model fit has significantly improved over the null model. In large data sets many parameters are statistically significant, even small and unimportant ones. The deviance seems to be a better way to judge model improvement. But again, with large data sets every little change causes the model to improve significantly.

As we illustrated in the sessions in this chapter, adding variables can change parameter estimates, while the model fit does not change. Changes in parameter estimates can be dramatic, as exemplified in the last session. Especially in small data sets, adding cross-level interactions can cause instability, with large standard errors as the symptoms. If we talk about small data sets in multilevel analyses we mean a small number of contexts rather than a small number of individual observations. After all, a data set with $n = 519$ is usually not considered to be that small. Still the differences between our reduced data set and the full one are considerable, especially for standard errors (as expected) and for second-level estimates. We want to stress again that in multilevel analysis practice there is a tendency to expand the data set, by adding interactions and contextual variables such as means. Data reduction is a very necessary strategy before starting any multilevel analyses. Multilevel analysis is not a tool for exploring large numbers of variables. Multilevel analysis is a nice tool for exploring small numbers of variables and making small changes in the models one at a time. As we have illustrated in this chapter, a small change in the way we treat the data can sometimes cause a large change in results.

Notes

1   By basic variables we mean all variables that are present in the data, which excludes the variables constructed later, such as interactions and aggregates such as means.
2   In addition to the notational convention outlined in note 2 of Chapter 2, we now also have to distinguish the variable from the label we use in MLn, with its restriction to eight characters. The MLn label is used in boxed MLn instructions, and it is written without capitals and in a non-proportional font, as in math.
3   The data are made available in this book as a service to the reader. They can be used to practice the execution of multilevel analyses in general and the use of MLn in particular.
4   The intercept is called a 'variable' in this context, even though it is a constant. All observations have the same value.
5   This means that a variance component is defined corresponding to the variable.
6   In this book explanatory variables vary only at a higher level than the level at which they are measured. An exception is the coefficient for the intercept cons. MLn allows users to declare coefficients random at their own level, as well as at a higher level. The option to allow coefficients to be random at their own level is not discussed in this book. This issue goes well beyond the scope of multilevel analysis.
7   Two R^2s in two-level analyses, but of course three R^2s with three levels, etc. It is assumed that errors across levels are uncorrelated. More about the calculation, the use, and the meaning of the two different R^2s in two-level analyses can be found in Chapter 5.
8   The between variance becomes complicated when random slopes are also present, as discussed earlier.
9   Fixed, as opposed to random. 'Fixed' means that we do not assume that the effect of 'HomeWork' on math achievement is different among schools.
10 The correlation can be calculated by dividing the covariance -26.14 by the product of the standard deviations of slope and intercept.
11 First-time users of multilevel modeling may be confused what a second-level or context variable is. Conceptually variables may be defined as context variables, as in the case of 'ParentEducation', but that does not qualify such variables as second-level variables in a multilevel analysis, where the second level, or context, is defined explicitly (remember that the levels are defined as student and school in our analyses). The level to which a variable belongs in a multilevel analysis can best be assessed by looking at the data matrix. If a variable is the same within the defined context (the school in our example), and has no variation within that context (all observations within the same school have the same score for that variable), then the variable is by definition a second-level variable. 'ParentEducation' is by that definition a student-level variable, not a context variable. The context is in our example defined as the school, and students in the same school have by no means equal values for the variable 'ParentEducation'. Of course, the variable 'ParentEducation' could be changed into a school-level variable by aggregation. Aggregation can be done in many ways. The commonest way is to calculate a mean parental education for each school. Note that the opposite is also true. A variable that has different values within the second level is a first-level variable.

12 Note that in MLn coefficients can be made random at the same level as they are measured. This can be easily accomplished by adding a statement to set the variance for that variable at level 2 (SETV 2 'schsize'). This special option of MLn is not discussed here. In this book we assume that users want to set variances for coefficients at a level higher than the level of measurement. In multilevel analyses the coefficients for 'SchoolSize' and 'SchoolSector' would only be allowed to be random if a third level were present in the data. An example of a third level for our data could be states of the USA. In that case we have three levels, where students are nested in schools, and schools are nested in different states. If we were interested in the effects of states on schools we could allow coefficients of school-level explanatory variables to differ over states. An analysis that fits up to three levels needs large data sets. For instance in our example, dividing our 23 schools over the 50 states of the USA would be a pointless exercise.

5 FREQUENTLY ASKED QUESTIONS

5.1 Introduction

Although the multilevel model is fairly restrictive, it is an important and non-trivial generalization of the usual linear regression model. This means that questions such as stability of regression coefficients, influence of multi-collinearity, and testing of model assumptions, which are already problematic in large multiple regression models, become even more complicated in multilevel models. Furthermore, a host of new questions are introduced that are specific to multilevel models. And some of the classical questions require new, or modified, answers, because of the specific structure of the multilevel model. Examples are the centering of explanatory variables and the consequences of dealing with multiple sources of variation. Because of the hierarchical nature of the data, and the fact that multilevel models have cross-level interactions, the discussion of centering explanatory variables is especially relevant, and different from the usual case. The fact that there are multiple sources of variation, on multiple levels, makes it complicated to define 'explained' or 'modeled' variance in a unique way. Again, this is a complication which simply does not occur in single-level or contextual models.

To pay tribute to the growing importance of the Internet, we will present this chapter in the form of a list of 'frequently asked questions'. In compiling our FAQs we have made extensive use of the questions asked on the multilevel mailing list,[1] which often shows quite clearly what researchers using multilevel analysis are interested in. Because of the availability of multilevel software, researchers are now able to fit complicated models, but they may have problems with interpreting certain features of the output. The following six questions will be addressed.

1 What are the effects of transforming the explanatory variables to deviations from the grand mean or to deviations from the group mean?
2 How is 'explained variance' defined in hierarchical linear models? Is there an analog to the multiple correlation coefficient? In particular, can we say how much of the variation in the outcome is 'due' to group factors, and how much to individual factors? What happens to the various quantities we estimate if we add more variables?
3 What can we say about the power of regression analyses if we use hierarchical linear models?

4   A coefficient in a multilevel analysis can be non-random and constant for all groups, it can be non-random and variable over groups, and it can be random (which also means, of course, that it is variable). What does it mean to choose either one of these options, and what are the consequences of changing from one option to another?

5   What are FIML, REML, EM, IGLS, RIGLS, EB/ML, OLS, GLS?

6   How serious is the problem of multicollinearity in multilevel analysis?

The chapter is necessarily more methodological and technical than previous chapters, but we emphasize concepts and not formal mathematical manipulations. Where possible, we refer to the results and examples discussed earlier.

5.2   The effects of centering

Frequently Asked Question 1. What are the effects of transforming the explanatory variables to deviations from the grand mean or to deviations from the group mean?

The effects of centering will be illustrated using the large NELS-88 data set as in some of the examples in Chapter 4. We will argue that an answer to the centering question is not simple, since the effect depends on the relationships in the data and on the goals of the analysis. Researchers tend to believe that data manipulation in multilevel analysis has effects similar to traditional regression analysis, where addition or subtraction of a constant does not change the relationships in the data. For that reason the discussion starts with a summary of the known effects of centering in a traditional analysis. Then we proceed by showing that centering in multilevel regression has different and sometimes unexpected effects, depending on the way the variables are centered.

5.2.1   Centering in fixed effects regression models

The effects of centering for traditional regression models are summarized in Aiken and West (1991), where 'centering' means subtracting the same value from each score of any explanatory variable. That value is usually the grand mean, but it could be any other value. In general, it is clear that subtracting the same value from each score does not essentially change the relations in the data. Simple additive transformations of a variable have no effect on the variance of that variable, nor on its covariances and correlations with other variables in the model, as long as the model contains only first-order terms (Aiken and West, 1991). In ordinary fixed effects regression the intercept is retained as a free parameter in order to guarantee invariance of the model with respect to the shift of origin of the explanatory variables. Consequently, centering (i.e. putting scores in deviation form) does not change the magnitude of the regression coefficients, only the magnitude of the intercept. This invariance of the coefficients occurs for any value added to or subtracted from the original variables. At the same time the change in intercept value is directly related to the value added or subtracted.[2]

The practical purpose of centering an explanatory variable in traditional fixed effect linear models is to change the interpretation of the intercept. Using deviation scores instead of raw scores affects the value of the intercept, and also, more importantly, its interpretation. In raw score models the intercept is the value of the response variable when all the explanatory variables are zero. In social science regression problems, such as those using attitude or intelligence tests, variables have no meaningful zero. In such instances, centering explanatory variables renders the intercept meaningful as the value of the response variable at the mean of all explanatory variables.

5.2.2 Centering in multilevel models

We refer to Kreft *et al.* (1995) for a more technical answer to this FAQ. Here we follow a slightly different route. First a model is investigated that has only one first-level explanatory variable x, a random intercept, and a random slope. A second-level variable z is part of the model, interacting with the intercept as well as with the slope. Thus we have the fairly general multilevel model

$$\underline{y}_{ij} = \underline{\alpha}_j + \underline{\beta}_j x_{ij} + \underline{\varepsilon}_{ij}, \tag{5.1a}$$

$$\underline{\alpha}_j = \alpha + \gamma_0 z_j + \underline{\delta}_{0j}, \tag{5.1b}$$

$$\underline{\beta}_j = \beta + \gamma_1 z_j + \underline{\delta}_{1j}. \tag{5.1c}$$

If we make the necessary substitutions we can write out the three equations (5.1) in a single-equation form. We have done this in previous chapters. The result for the fixed part is

$$\mathbf{E}(\underline{y}_{ij}) = \alpha + \beta x_{ij} + \gamma_0 z_j + \gamma_1 x_{ij} z_j, \tag{5.2a}$$

and for the random part

$$\underline{y}_{ij} - \mathbf{E}(\underline{y}_{ij}) = \underline{\delta}_{0j} + x_{ij}\underline{\delta}_{1j} + \underline{\varepsilon}_{ij}. \tag{5.2b}$$

Our discussion centers around the student-level variable x_{ij}, which is in raw score form in equation (5.1). This variable can be used in a grand mean centered form, where x_{ij} is replaced by $\ddot{x}_{ij}$, which is the deviation from the grand mean $\ddot{x}_{ij} = x_{ij} - \overline{x}$. Using this centered score instead of the raw score will yield a model that is equivalent to the raw score model when we add this subtracted mean to the model. Since the subtracted mean is a constant (the same mean is subtracted from all scores) it gets absorbed by the intercept α. As a result the grand mean centered model is related to the raw score model in a simple way.

The effect of subtracting the grand mean is much simpler than when the group means are subtracted from the scores. Group means are most likely not equal among groups, and different numbers will be subtracted from some scores than from others. The group mean centered score $\tilde{x}_{ij}$ is equal to $\tilde{x}_{ij} = x_{ij} - \bar{x}_j$. Using this centered score instead of the raw score will yield a model that is no longer equivalent to the raw score model. We can reestablish equivalence if we add the subtracted mean back into the model, as an important between-group effect. In such cases the mean is treated in the same way as any second-level variable is, as shown in the following equation:

$$\underline{\alpha}_j = \alpha + \gamma_{01}\bar{x}_j + \gamma_{02}z_j + \underline{\delta}_{0j}. \tag{5.3}$$

That this addition of the mean has consequences for some of the parameter estimates in the model will be discussed and illustrated with examples.

We will also indicate that statistical equivalence no longer applies when random slopes are added. But even if models are statistically equivalent they do not give identical parameter estimates. For all practical purposes group mean centered models are different from raw score models. We emphasize that using group mean centering instead of raw scores serves different purposes and tests different theories.

5.2.3 Grand mean centering

We first study what happens to the model if we center the explanatory variable around the overall mean. For this purpose, we use the decomposition of the explanatory variable as the sum of the centered variable and its overall mean or *grand mean*. If we substitute x_{ij} in equations (5.2a) and (5.2b) by the sum of the deviation score $\ddot{x}_{ij}$ and the grand mean $\bar{x}$, and collect terms with corresponding subscripts, we find, after some tedious algebra, that two fixed coefficients change, the value of the intercept α and the value of the second-level coefficient γ_0. Weighted values, $\beta\bar{x}$ and $\gamma_1\bar{x}$, of the grand mean are added to α and γ_0 respectively. These changes are indicated in the following equation within the brackets:

$$\mathbf{E}(\underline{y}_{ij}) = [\alpha + \beta\bar{x}] + \beta\ddot{x}_{ij} + [\gamma_0 + \gamma_1\bar{x}]z_j + \gamma_1\ddot{x}_{ij}z_j. \tag{5.4a}$$

Equation (5.4a) shows that a constant is added in both cases. It is easy and straightforward to calculate the raw score coefficients from the grand mean centered coefficients. In any analysis where grand mean centering is used the pre-centered values for the two coefficients can be obtained by subtracting the mean (weighted by either the β or γ_1) from the parameter estimates of α and γ_0.

Another observed change among the two models is the value of the variance of the intercept. This variance changes with a value again directly related to the (subtracted) mean. Similar to equation (5.4a), we now have

$$\underline{y}_{ij} - \mathbf{E}(\underline{y}_{ij}) = (\underline{\delta}_{0j} + \bar{x}\underline{\delta}_{1j}) + \ddot{x}_{ij}\underline{\delta}_{1j} + \underline{\varepsilon}_{ij}. \tag{5.4b}$$

It can be shown that using raw scores or grand mean centered scores does not change the model, but it does change the values of some of the parameters. Comparing equation (5.2a) with equation (5.4a) and equation (5.2b) with equation (5.4b) shows that they describe precisely the same model, the first one with the raw x_{ij} as the explanatory variable, the second with the centered $\ddot{x}_{ij}$.

It is quite easy to transform one model into the other. In the terminology used by Kreft *et al.* (1995), the raw score model and the grand mean centered model are *equivalent linear models*. This does *not* mean that all parameter estimates are actually equal. Equivalent models will give the same fit, the same predicted values, and the same residuals, while the parameter estimates can easily be translated into each other.

5.2.4 Group mean centering

Now let us see what happens if we replace the raw scores x_{ij} by the group mean centered scores $\tilde{x}_{ij} = x_{ij} - \bar{x}_j$, where $\bar{x}_j$ are the group means. Proceeding in the same way as in Section 5.2.3, we substitute $x_{ij} = \tilde{x}_{ij} + \bar{x}_j$ in (5.5), and collect terms. This shows a similar change in parameter estimates to that in the grand mean centered model, although we need to replace the grand mean with the group mean in equation (5.4a), which gives

$$\mathbf{E}(\underline{y}_{ij}) = [\alpha + \beta\bar{x}_j] + \beta\tilde{x}_{ij} + [\gamma_0 + \gamma_1\bar{x}_j]z_j + \gamma_1\tilde{x}_{ij}z_j; \qquad (5.5a)$$

for the random part we have

$$\underline{y}_{ij} - \mathbf{E}(\underline{y}_{ij}) = (\underline{\delta}_{0j} + \bar{x}_j\underline{\delta}_{1j}) + \tilde{x}_{ij}\underline{\delta}_{1j} + \underline{\varepsilon}_{ij}. \qquad (5.5b)$$

Equation (5.5a) shows again that the intercept and the coefficient for the second-level variable z_j are affected. The problem is that it is no longer possible to bring this form back to the raw score form as we did before. The mean in equation (5.5a) is not a single value, as the grand mean is, but varies over groups. As a result, different values will be subtracted from the intercept α in each group, and no unique value exists. The same is true for the value of the coefficient for z in equation (5.5a), and for the variance of the intercept in equation (5.5b).

As a result the group mean centered model and the raw score model are equivalent neither in the fixed part nor in the random part. This is true for all situations except in two special cases. One exception is the case where $\bar{x}_j$ is equal to $\bar{x}$ in all groups. This happens in repeated measures analysis, but it is a rare situation for researchers interested in group differences, such as school effects.

The other situation where we find equivalence of group mean centered and raw score models is a model with only a random intercept, with slopes that are constant (not random), and in which the group means are reintroduced as second-level variables. This leads to some major simplifications. We find that $\gamma_1 = 0$, the slope is fixed and thus $\underline{\delta}_{1j} = 0$, and $z_j = \bar{x}_j$. Fitting such a model turns out to be the same as fitting a raw score model with only a random intercept, but without the means as second-level variable. These two simplified models are equivalent. Again values obtained with the centered model can easily be translated to those of the raw score model.

5.2.5 An example

A substantial body of research (Coleman *et al.*, 1982) reports positive effects of the private sector on students' achievement. One such effect is that the private sector is more egalitarian than the public sector. We look into this problem, using the NELS-88 data set, in this subsection. By using centered and raw score models we show that answers to these questions do not always agree. They depend on the way explanatory variables are treated, as centered within contexts (CWC) or as raw scores (RS).

The results of Raudenbush and Bryk's (1986) analysis with the 'High School and Beyond' data show that the private sector has an effect on the relationship between 'SES' and 'MathAchievement'. This cross-level inter-action between the school-level variable 'SchoolSector' and the student-level variable 'SES' showed a significant effect, indicating that the Catholic sector is slightly more egalitarian: 'lower-SES students fare better in Catholic schools, and higher-SES students fare better in public schools' (Raudenbush and Bryk, 1986, p. 13). In our replication of Raudenbush and Bryk's CWC model, we again use the NELS-88 data with 21 580 students and 1003 schools, with the same goal, to evaluate the merits of the private school sector compared to the public sector. The model used is the familiar one, where 'MathAchievement' is predicted by the student-level explanatory variables, 'HomeWork' and 'SES'. In our NELS-88 data most schools are in the public sector (80%). The remaining 20% is divided over Catholic schools (10%), religious private schools (4%), and non-religious private schools (6%). In Raudenbush and Bryk's model the variables are CWC, while we fit both a CWC and an RS model and discuss the different results.

In the analyses three different models are fitted to the data, using the same explanatory variables 'HomeWork' and 'SES', but centered and added to the model in different ways. The second-level variable 'Public' is always present in the model, while some models have the second-level variable 'Ratio', which measures the student–teacher ratio. Three fairly common models are used: an RS model, a CWC model without the group means reintroduced as second-level variables, and a CWC model with means added back to the model.

The models are sometimes incorrectly believed to be equivalent, even when CWC models are used without reintroducing the subtracted mean back into the model. In this last model, the between-group variation of the centered variable is deleted. This between-group variation may play an important role, as we show in our examples, where the subtraction of the mean and thus the deletion of the between variation in the variables 'HomeWork' and 'SES' has important consequences for the 'Public' school effect (see Tables 5.1 and 5.2). In both tables the distinction is made between an RS model, a CWC model without reintroduced means, CWC(N), and a CWC model with reintroduction of the subtracted means, CWC(M). This last way of treating the data is used by Raudenbush and Bryk.

Table 5.1   Effects on 'Public' of different treatments of the data (note that underlined variables are centered as opposed to raw score variables)

	RS		CWC(N)		CWC(M)	
	EST	SE	EST	SE	EST	SE
Intercept	50.16	0.28	55.06	0.35	47.53	0.47
'HomeWork'	1.24	0.05	n.a		n.a	
'HomeWork'	n.a		1.18	0.05	1.20	0.05
'SES'	4.35	0.09	n.a		n.a	
'SES'	n.a		3.84	0.10	3.85	0.10
'Public'	−2.06	0.29	−5.42	0.39	+0.62	0.28
'MeanSES'	n.a		n.a		8.14	0.25
'MeanHomeWork'	n.a		n.a		1.65	0.20
Variance slope 'SES'	0.47	0.33	1.65	0.44	1.71	0.44
Deviance	153 333		153 968		153 004	

The centered variables are indicated in the tables by underlining, as in 'HomeWork' or 'SES'. For instance 'HomeWork' is used in the RS model, while 'HomeWork' is used in both CWC models. All models have one school-level explanatory variable, 'Public', where private schools are coded as 0 and public as 1. Note that the third model in Table 5.1 contains two more school-level variables, the two subtracted means of 'MeanSES' and 'MeanHomeWork'. In the RS model the means are not fitted since they are not subtracted from the raw scores, and are still present in the model. The models in Table 5.1 are fitted with a random slope for SES and homework.

As Table 5.1 shows, the results of the RC model are not the same as the results of both CWC models, either in the values of the coefficients, or in the goodness of fit, the deviances. That the results of CWC(N) and CWC(M) differ is caused by the deletion of the between-school variance of the variables 'HomeWork' and 'SES' in the CWC(N) model, where the means are subtracted from the raw scores and not reintroduced again. For that reason the RS model is more comparable to the CWC(M) than to the CWC(N) model, which is also indicated by the goodness of fit: the CWC(N) model has the largest deviance.

The differences in the fixed effects are mainly present in the second-level variable for the coefficient of 'Public' and in the value of the intercept. The estimates for 'HomeWork' (raw and centered) and for 'SES' (raw and centered) are very close, with equal standard errors. In the random part, of which we only show the variance of the variable 'SES', the difference between RS and the two CWC models leads to opposite conclusions. The magnitudes of all three estimates of the variance of the slope for 'SES' are different, while the standard errors are very close. In the RS model this variance is not significant, while in both CWC models it is significant.

A similar thing happens with the fixed effect for 'Public': this effect is large and negative in the RS model, where we find a coefficient of −2.06; is even larger in the first CWC model, where we find an effect of -5.42; but changes sign in the last CWC model, where it becomes $+0.62$, a small but significant effect. All three effects are statistically significant, but unequal in magnitude and, more importantly, unequal in sign. The conclusion is that, depending on how the raw data are treated, a negative effect for the public sector can be changed to a positive effect for that sector. In our example centering has a clear effect. Centering without reintroducing the means favors the private sector, as shown in the CWC(N) model where the effect is -5.42, up from -2.06 in the RS model. Centering with the means reintroduced favors the public sector, where the effect size for 'Public' reverses sign and becomes positive 0.62. The favorable effect for the public sector is a direct result of the introduction of the means, which provides a correction for the difference among sectors in 'SES' and 'HomeWork'.

The models in Table 5.1 are not equivalent, which is also indicated by differences in deviances. The three models do not fit the data equally well. The CWC(N) model has the highest deviance, and thus the worst fit to the data. This is not surprising since the important between variation of the variables 'SES' and 'HomeWork' is deleted from the CWC(N) model. The other striking difference among the models is in the random part, where the slope for 'SES' is not significantly random in the RS model, while it is significantly random in both CWC models. This finding has consequences for further data analyses, as we will discuss next.

5.2.6   Cross-level interactions with 'Public' and 'SES'

In the RS model we conclude that the relationship between 'SES' and 'MathAchievement' is not significantly different among schools, since the slope for 'SES' is not significantly random. As a result we will not try to 'explain' the variation of 'SES' by means of a school characteristic such as 'Public' or 'Ratio', since we believe, based on this result, that such variation does not exist. But the significant variance of the slope for 'SES' in both CWC models is an invitation to explore whether differences in the relationship among schools between 'SES' and math achievement can be explained by sector differences. A new model is fitted where cross-level interactions between 'Public' and 'SES', and between 'Public' and 'HomeWork', are added to our previous CWC models. The results for the fixed effects with the three models, RS, CWC(N) and CWC(M), are given in Table 5.2. Again 'SES' and 'HomeWork' are the student-level explanatory variables, either as raw scores or as centered (underlined) scores. The school-level explanatory variables are the same dummy variable for sector, 'Public', and a variable indicating class size, expressed as teacher/student ratio, 'Ratio'. All models have a random intercept and random slopes for 'SES' and 'HomeWork', with the exception of the RS model, where 'SES' has a fixed slope, since the RS model in Table 5.1 showed that the slope of 'SES' is not significantly random. For the same reason as discussed before, the

Table 5.2 Cross-level interactions in RS and CWC

	RS		CWC(N)		CWC(M)	
	EST	SE	EST	SE	EST	SE
Intercept	54.00	0.57	60.30	0.68	48.74	0.65
'HomeWork'	0.86	0.10	n.a		n.a	
'HomeWork'	n.a		0.76	0.10	0.80	0.10
'SES'	4.30	0.09	n.a		n.a	
'SES'	n.a		2.96	0.26	2.97	0.26
'Public'	−3.35	0.37	−5.57	0.38	0.44	0.29
'Ratio'	−0.16	0.02	−0.29	0.03	−0.06	0.02
'MeanHomeWork'	n.a		n.a		1.62	0.20
'MeanSES'	n.a		n.a		7.98	0.25
'Public' × 'HomeWork'	0.48	0.11	0.53	0.11	0.51	0.11
'Public' × 'SES'	n.a		1.03	0.28	1.03	0.28
Deviance	153272		153853		152963	

RS model in Table 5.2 has no cross-level interaction with 'SES', such as the interaction 'Public' × 'SES'.

The results of the analyses show again the consequences of centering. Models without means at the second level, which are the RS model and the CWC(N) model, enhance school-level effects of 'Public' and 'Ratio'. The strong effect for 'Public' in the RS model of −3.35 has a z-score of 9.05. The effect of 'Public' is even larger in the CWC(N) model, with a magnitude of −5.57 and a z-score of 14.7. But in the CWC(M) model the effect of 'Public' becomes positive, and is no longer significant, with a z-score of 1.52. The magnitude of the school-level coefficient for 'Ratio' is affected in a similar way. In the RS model it has a magnitude of −0.16 with a z-score of 8, in the CWC(N) model it is enhanced to −0.29 with a z-score of 9.67, while in the CWC(M) model it is lower again, with a magnitude of −0.06 and a z-score of 3. The change of the value of the coefficients for school-level variables shows again that adding or deleting means to a CWC model may affect school-level coefficients.

Data manipulation, such as centering and adding or deleting means, has consequences. Different conclusions can be drawn from one model compared to the other regarding the school-level effects, while the student-level effects are hardly affected and very similar over models.

We are left to ask which is the correct model. This question cannot be answered on the basis of technical considerations alone, since all three models in Table 5.2 are 'correct'. The choice needs to be made based on the researcher's knowledge of the data and the goals of the analysis. If the researcher is mostly interested in a model that 'explains' as much variation in the response variable as possible, without any particular interest in second-level effects, fitting an RS model will be the easiest way to go. No choices need to be made about reintroducing means, since no means are removed to start with. The RS model is also best if the researcher is more interested in the effects on individual students' performance than in school effects.

The choice of a CWC model is based on a distinct interest in separating individual effects from school effects, with an underlying idea that two separate models are tested: an individual student model and a school-level model. In that situation the decision to center and not to add the mean to the model is based on theory. If theory indicates, in our example, that the mean level of 'SES' and/or 'HomeWork' is a sector characteristic, the question remains whether that characteristic needs to be controlled for before any comparison between sectors can be made. As is illustrated, it does make a difference.

It is up to the researcher to fit either a RS, a CWC(N), or a CWC(M) model. We have illustrated that this choice is an important one, and may not be easy to make. Centering is good for technical purposes, since it removes high correlations between random intercept and slopes, and high correlations between first- and second-level variables and cross-level interactions (see Section 5.7). Centering stabilizes the model, and allows one to look at coefficients as more or less independent estimates. Statistically we know that centered models are more stable models, for instance by deleting the correlation between the centered first-level (= student) and second-level (= school) variables. On the other hand, centering is fitting another model, a model that may not fulfill the requirements of the investigation.

As we discussed in Chapter 2, a contextual model can be fitted with and without centering. That discussion related to fixed coefficient models, and showed how the total variance can be divided up in several ways. Depending on the way the data are treated (as centered) or not treated (as raw scores) the interpretation of the coefficient for the context effect changes. In the raw score model the context effect is defined in Chapter 2 as $b_W - b_B$, while the centered context effect is b_B. In RC models centering has this same effect, plus an effect on the random coefficients. In fixed as well as in RC models the decision to center or not to center is, however, still the same; it needs to be decided from situation to situation. If one decides to center, the only advice we can give in this book is to add the subtracted mean to the model. If this is not done, and a CWC(N) model is fitted, an uncorrected between-schools effect is measured. This between effect is not corrected for the mean effect of the centered first-level explanatory variables. This may be exactly what one wants, as in growth curve models, where the explanatory variable is time.

By showing the consequences of the choices in centering, and by illustrating it based on a real data set and a realistic research question, we hope to have attracted the attention of researchers to this problem. Our illustration may give researchers reasons to think hard before applying centering merely because they desire statistical stability. If centering is used for the right reasons it does indeed carry the reward of less confounding of the parameter estimates. This gain is equally large for fixed as well as for random coefficient models.

5.3 Modeled variance

Frequently Asked Question 2. How is 'explained variance' or R^2 defined in hierarchical linear models? Is there an analog to the multiple correlation coefficient? In particular, can we say how much of the variation in the outcome is 'due' to group factors, and how much to individual factors? What happens to the various quantities we estimate if we add more variables?

It is interesting, from the user's point of view, to redefine the classical notions of 'multiple correlation' and 'explained variance'[3] in multilevel models. Unfortunately, this is not simple, since two different versions of the between variance can be defined, written below as τ^2 and ω^2. This last definition of the between variance is used by Snijders and Bosker (1994). Using one or other definition results in different estimates for the within as well as for the between modeled variance. We do not discuss which of the two ways of calculating R^2s is most valuable or most correct, since the concept has rather limited use in multilevel modeling. It is well defined in group mean centered models and models with random intercept only. The main reason for the limited use is that it cannot be uniquely defined in models with random slopes.

The development of our discussion builds on Snijders and Bosker (1994), where the discussion of modeled variance is related to that of centering (see Section 5.2).

In ordinary least squares, without any partitioning into groups, we could fit the standard regression model with a single explanatory variable x_{ij}, given by

$$\underline{y}_{ij} = a + b x_{ij} + \underline{\varepsilon}_{ij}. \tag{5.6}$$

The error term, $\underline{\varepsilon}_{ij}$, has a mean of zero and variance σ^2. The maximum likelihood estimate of the parameter σ^2 is the variance of the residuals. To put it another way, the residual sum of squares around the fitted regression line estimates the residual variance.

We also have the familiar analysis of variance table, in which the sum of squares 'due to regression' and the sum of squared 'residuals due to regression' add up to the total variance of the $\underline{y}_{ij}$. The same is true for the 'contextual' models of Chapter 2, in which the estimation technique is always OLS (although with different sets of explanatory variables). In all these examples there is only one variance component parameter in the model, and it is estimated by the sum of squares of the residuals. It continues to make sense to call one component the modeled variance, or to define the squared multiple correlation coefficient as the proportion of variance due to regression.

But even in this simplest of contexts, the approach (and perhaps the terminology) already gets us into trouble if we wish to say how much of the modeled variance is 'due' to the first explanatory variable, how much to the second explanatory variable, and so on. For uncorrelated explanatory variables, which basically only exist in balanced design experiments, the modeled variance is the sum of squares of the regression coefficients. Thus the square of the regression coefficient of a variable is the variance modeled by that variable. But this scheme fails miserably with correlated explanatory variables, leading to endless discussion on how much variation is 'explained' by genes and how much by environment, or how much by race and how much by socio-economic status. Social scientists have proposed various ways out of this dilemma, but those that stay within the regression paradigm are not very convincing. And, as we shall see below, life becomes considerably more complicated if the multilevel model is true, and/or if we use multilevel techniques to estimate the parameters.

5.3.1 Random intercept models

By now the equations of random coefficient models are familiar, with the underlining of random variables. A random intercept model is again defined by

$$\underline{y}_{ij} = \underline{\alpha}_j + \beta x_{ij} + \underline{\varepsilon}_{ij}, \tag{5.7a}$$

where the intercept is related to a second-level variable z,

$$\underline{\alpha}_j = \alpha + \gamma z_j + \underline{\delta}_j. \tag{5.7b}$$

The two equations each show an error term, where the variance of the residuals at the first (= student) level, $\underline{\varepsilon}_{ij}$, is σ^2, and the variance of the residuals at the second (= school) level, $\underline{\delta}_j$, is τ^2. If these two variances summed to some meaningful total variance, our problem could be easily solved. But unfortunately, the two variances are confounded in the between part, as we will show when we discuss the equation for the deviance.

In the model the deviance Δ is given by

$$\Delta = m \log \omega^2 + m(n-1) \log \sigma^2 + \frac{SSQ_B(\gamma, \beta)}{\omega^2} + \frac{SSQ_W(\beta)}{\sigma^2}. \tag{5.8}$$

In this somewhat complex equation m is the number of groups, n the number of observations within groups. For convenience we assume that the design is balanced, that is to say, we have m groups of size n. SSQ_B is the sum of squares between, and equally SSQ_W is the sum of squares within. The quantity ω^2 is the 'total between' variance, which is defined as the sum of the variance within and n times the variance between: $\omega^2 = \sigma^2 + n\tau^2$.

For convenience we also assume that all variables are expressed as deviations from the grand mean, so we can forget about α, the fixed part of $\underline{\alpha}_j$ in equation (5.7). To explain why the two variances are confounded we employ deviation scores, using $\tilde{x}_{ij}$ and $\tilde{y}_{ij}$ for deviations from the group mean, and $\bar{x}_j$ and $\bar{y}_j$ for group means. The within sum of squares is defined as

$$SSQ_W(\beta) = \sum_{j=1}^{m} \sum_{i=1}^{n} (\tilde{y}_{ij} - \beta \tilde{x}_{ij})^2, \tag{5.9a}$$

while the between sum of squares is defined as

$$SSQ_B(\gamma, \beta) = n \sum_{j=1}^{m} (\bar{y}_j - \gamma z_j - \beta \bar{x}_j)^2. \qquad (5.9b)$$

What these equations tell us is that the second-level regression coefficient γ only occurs in the between sum of squares, but the first-level coefficient β occurs in both. This is a form of *confounding*: we cannot nicely separate the parameters into between and within parts.

Equation (5.8) also shows that the deviance is a weighted sum of the two residual sums of squares, with weights given by the variance components. But we observe more confounding: the between-group sum of squares $SSQ_B(\gamma, \beta)$, the third term in (5.8), gives information about ω^2, and thus about both σ^2 and τ^2. Both the within and between sums of squares give information about β (see the last two terms in equation (5.8)). This reflects the fact, already discussed in Chapter 2, that the regression coefficient β has a between as well as a within component. It is clear from equation (5.8) that SSQ_W and SSQ_B are confounded in β. This confounding is not present when x is expressed in terms of deviations from the group mean. In such cases all $\bar{x}_j$ are zero, and consequently β does not occur in $SSQ_B(\gamma, \beta)$, and the maximum likelihood estimate $\hat{\beta}$ of β is simply b_W. Alternatively, as we saw in Section 5.2, we can add the group mean as a second-level explanatory variable. This means that $\bar{x}_j$ gets its own regression coefficient, and we still have $\hat{\beta} = b_W$.

After the computation of the maximum likelihood estimates of β and γ, the variance component maximum likelihood estimates are calculated. Again we need some formulas to illustrate the definition of the variance within and the variance between:

$$\hat{\sigma}^2 = \frac{1}{m(n-1)} SSQ_W(\hat{\beta}), \qquad (5.10a)$$

$$\hat{\omega}^2 = \frac{1}{m} SSQ_B(\hat{\gamma}, \hat{\beta}). \qquad (5.10b)$$

Above we defined the total between variance as ω^2, where $\omega^2 = \sigma^2 + n\tau^2$, which implies that the intercept variance (or the between-group variance) τ^2 is estimated by

$$\hat{\tau}^2 = \frac{\hat{\omega}^2 - \hat{\sigma}^2}{n}. \qquad (5.10c)$$

This formula works provided that the $\hat{\tau}^2$ thus defined is non-negative. We run into problems if $\hat{\sigma}^2 > \hat{\omega}^2$, which results in $\hat{\tau}^2 < 0$, which of course does not make sense.

5.3.2 Using the null model as a way to calculate R^2

In the analyses of Chapter 4 we sometimes used the null model to define what we mean by multiple correlation and 'explained' variance in multilevel models. The null model is defined as a model with a random intercept only. The intercept has error terms at both levels, the second level ($\underline{\delta}_j$) and the first level ($\underline{\varepsilon}_{ij}$). Thus

$$\underline{y}_{ij} = \alpha + \underline{\delta}_j + \underline{\varepsilon}_{ij}. \tag{5.11}$$

The variances of the error terms are the variance components $\hat{\tau}_0^2$, which defines the between variance, and $\hat{\sigma}_0^2$, which defines the within variance. In the balanced case, $\hat{\tau}_0^2$ is simply SSW_B, while $\hat{\sigma}_0^2 = SSQ_W$.

If we fit more elaborate random intercept models, by adding variables, we find new variance component estimates, $\hat{\tau}_1^2$ and $\hat{\sigma}_1^2$. Using the estimates for the variance components obtained by the null model and subtracting the newly found variance components, we hope to find a reduction in error variance. For instance, in our data we expect that the addition of a student-level variable will mainly reduce the within-schools variance, that a group mean centered score will only reduce the within-schools variance, and that a school-level explanatory variable will only reduce the between-schools variance. A reduction of error variance at one or other level can be stated in a percentage reduction, which is the value for 'explained variance' or R^2. The calculation of the two R^2s, using the null model, can be done by using the equations (5.12) for R_B^2 as well as for R_W^2:

$$\hat{R}_B^2 = \frac{\hat{\tau}_0^2 - \hat{\tau}_1^2}{\hat{\tau}_0^2}, \tag{5.12a}$$

$$\hat{R}_W^2 = \frac{\hat{\sigma}_0^2 - \hat{\sigma}_1^2}{\hat{\sigma}_0^2}. \tag{5.12b}$$

These equations show that to calculate both R^2s we take the variance of the new model and subtract it from the variance of the null model. The difference is compared to the original variance (the null model variance) as a proportion reduction in that variance. This simple approach has its limitations, since it can lead to negative multiple correlation coefficients. As noted before, the $\hat{\tau}^2$ defined by (5.10c) can be negative. And, as mentioned in the introduction, it does not really apply to the case in which we have random slopes.

5.3.3   Using total between variance

By employing the definition of the total between variance $\hat{\omega}_1^2$ as used by Snijders and Bosker (1994), we will illustrate again what happens if we add a variable to the within and the between variance. First, we add a second-level variable. It has no within variation, so $\hat{\sigma}_1^2$ and $\hat{R}_W^2$ remain the same. But $\hat{\omega}_1^2$, the total between variance, is reduced and thus, because we know that $\hat{\omega}^2 = \hat{\sigma}^2 + n\hat{\tau}^2$, $\hat{\tau}_1^2$ is reduced as well. This means that $\hat{R}_B^2$ increases, which makes perfect sense.

If we add a variable with no between variation (i.e. in terms of deviations from the group mean), then $\hat{\sigma}_1^2$ decreases and $\hat{R}_W^2$ increases. Again, this makes sense. But $\hat{\omega}_1^2$ remains the same, which implies that $\hat{\tau}_1^2$ increases, and $\hat{R}_B^2$ defined by (5.12a) *decreases*. This is strange. We add a variable, without between-group variation, and the between-group multiple correlation coefficient becomes smaller. This is again because of confounding. If we were to define

$$\hat{R}_B^2 = \frac{\hat{\omega}_0^2 - \hat{\omega}_1^2}{\hat{\omega}_0^2} \tag{5.13}$$

instead, using the 'total between', then $\hat{R}_B^2$ would remain the same, which makes more sense. This is basically what Snijders and Bosker propose.

Generally, of course, variables will have both within-group and between-group variation. Thus both $\hat{\sigma}_1^2$ and $\hat{\omega}_1^2$ will become smaller, but it will still be the case that adding a variable with a small amount of between-group variation will tend to increase the estimate $\hat{\tau}_1^2$, and thus the intra-class correlation.

5.3.4 Conclusions

In this section we have shown that in multilevel models error variances can increase when a variable is added to the model. This is counter-intuitive, because we have learned to expect that adding a variable will decrease the error variance, or at least keep it at its current level. Reasons for an increase in SSQ_B and/or SSQ_W are discussed in the formulas of this section. It is shown that, given that ω^2 remains the same, changes in one part (in σ^2 or τ^2) induce changes in other part (τ^2 or σ^2). The confounding of SSQ_W and SSQ_B can be avoided by using group mean centered explanatory variables, with the subtracted means introduced separately as second-level explanatory variables. That this treatment of the data has consequences for the interpretation of the analysis is discussed in detail in Section 5.2. In general, we suggest not setting too much store by the calculation of an $\hat{R}_B^2$ or $\hat{R}_W^2$. Both concepts are ill defined and ambiguous, while their usefulness is limited to random intercept models.

5.4 Power

Frequently Asked Question 3. What can we say about the power of regression analyses if we use hierarchical linear models?

This question is far too general to be answered in a satisfactory way. The power functions shown in this section are only a few of the many power functions possible. The form of the function depends, among other things, on the null model. The null model, defined earlier as a model that divides the variance of the response variable into a within and a between part, can have low or high intra-class correlation. Compare again Table 1.1 in Chapter 1, where the work of Barcikowski is reported. This shows that size of the group in combination with the magnitude of the intra-class correlation have different effects on the power to reject the null-hypothesis, given that the assumed alpha level is set to 0.05.

Remember also that the power is the probability of rejecting the null hypothesis if it is *not* true. Thus power depends on the null hypothesis, but also on the particular way in which the null hypothesis is not true. Many of the assumptions of the null model can be violated, and each type of violation leads to a different 'power curve'. Assumptions that can be violated are:

- that the ε_{ij} are independent;
- that the ε_{ij} are normal with mean zero and constant variance σ^2;
- that all δ_j are also normal and independent, with mean zero and variance τ^2; and
- that the δ_j and ε_{ij} are independent.

Also power curves may differ depending on the estimation method used, the strength of the intra-class correlation, the strength of the effect, and the number of observations.

Let us start with a simple model again. The simplest non-trivial multilevel model is one with a random intercept only:

$$y_{ij} = \alpha_j + \beta x_{ij} + \varepsilon_{ij}, \tag{5.14a}$$

$$\alpha_j = \alpha + \delta_j. \tag{5.14b}$$

In order to discuss the power of a test for a particular effect – say the effect β – we need to define the deviation of the fitted and true models and the estimation method of β. Since power is defined as the probability of finding a significant effect, when such an effect is indeed present in the data, the test of significance is crucial here. The test of significance leans heavily on the standard error of the estimated β. Thus the estimated sampling variance of β determines the power of the regression model. If this sampling error is estimated to be small, the power is large; if the same sampling error is estimated to be larger, the power is smaller.

This will be demonstrated by discussing three different estimates of the sampling variance of $\hat{\beta}$. One estimate is the variance of the maximum likelihood estimate, $\mathbf{V}(\hat{\beta}_{ML})$. Another is a variance of the OLS estimate $\mathbf{V}(\hat{\beta}_{OLS})$ which has the correct variance for multilevel models, since it takes the intra-class correlation into account. The third is produced by the usual regression methods, where intra-class correlation is ignored, which is the OLS variance estimate V_{OLS}. We do not give the precise formulas here, because they are not very interesting. But it is possible to show that in general the 'incorrect' variance OLS estimate is the smallest, while the 'correct' OLS variance estimate is the largest. The maximum likelihood estimate lies in between:

$$\hat{V}_{OLS} \leq \mathbf{V}(\hat{\beta}_{ML}) \leq \mathbf{V}(\hat{\beta}_{OLS}). \tag{5.15}$$

One conclusion is that using the incorrect OLS estimate V_{OLS} gives the greatest power, as a direct result of having the smallest standard error. The trade-off is that it may not always be the best one to use. If we do not assume intra-class correlation when it is present, we *underestimate* the standard error of the regression coefficient. In that case we claim to have more precision than we really have. In consequence we are more likely to obtain a significant result, with the downside that we may falsely reject the null hypothesis. This has been demonstrated by Barcikowski (see Table 1.1 in Chapter 1), and will be illustrated again in Figure 5.1.

Thus we distinguish three choices for the standard error we may use in the significance test.

1. The OLS estimate of β has standard error $V(\hat{\beta}_{OLS})$. In the test we use $\hat{V}_{OLS}$, which is the wrong standard error (if the multilevel model is non-trivially true). Using these standard errors amounts to assuming that the intra-class correlation is zero, when it is not.
2. The OLS estimate of β is used with standard error $V(\hat{\beta}_{OLS})$, which means we use the correct standard error in this case, since it takes the intra-class correlation into account.
3. The maximum likelihood estimate of β is used with standard error $V(\hat{\beta}_{ML})$, which is also the correct standard error in this case.

5.4.1 Some simple cases

In this subsection the power for a simple test situation is studied, and we use a one-sided test of the null hypothesis that β is zero. Thus we reject H_0 at level $\alpha = 0.05$ if the computed $\hat{\beta}$, divided by its (known) standard error, is larger than $z(\alpha)$, say z equal to or larger than 1.96, the usual normal-theory significance level. Actually, we allow for the possibility of using the 'wrong' standard error. Let us make this a little clearer. If we compute $\hat{\beta}$ by maximum likelihood, then the correct standard error to use in the test is the square root of $V(\hat{\beta}_{ML})$. If we compute $\hat{\beta}$ by OLS, then we should use $V(\hat{\beta}_{OLS})$. But we may compute $\hat{\beta}$ by OLS and use V_{OLS}, which is not a correct estimate of the standard error in the multilevel model in equation (5.14). The probability that we reject H_0 (i.e. the power) is consequently the probability that $\hat{\beta}$, divided by the standard error we use in the test, is larger than $z(\alpha)$.

By computing the rejection probabilities for the three estimation methods we obtain three power functions, shown in Figure 5.1. The functions are based on one-sided testing in one specific situation. The example is one of many possible, where the intra-class correlation, the ratio of $V_B(x)$ to $V_T(x)$, is 0.50, and where $\omega^2 = 10$, $\sigma^2 = 1$, and $\alpha = 0.05$. The horizontal axis in the figure is the true value of β, and the vertical axis is the probability of rejection of the null hypothesis $\beta = 0$.

The figure should be read as follows. The rejection of the null hypothesis should happen whenever the 'true' value is larger than zero (one-sided test). The higher the probability of rejection of the null hypothesis when it should be rejected (i.e. when values are larger than zero), the higher the power of the

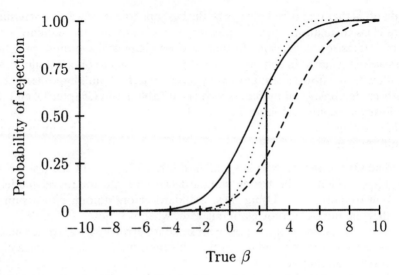

Figure 5.1   Power functions (probability of rejection as a function of β).

method. But equally important is the bias of the three methods, when chances are higher of wrongly rejecting the null hypothesis when the true β is zero. The three curves represent the three cases discussed earlier. The solid line shows the power of the test of the OLS estimate if we use the 'wrong' standard error. The dashed line represents OLS with a correct standard error, and the dotted line the maximum likelihood results, also with the correct standard error.

The figure shows that for all methods the probability of rejecting the null hypothesis increases with larger effects (the true β). Thus all three tests are consistent. But the three functions are not equal. The solid line, which is based on the OLS estimate with incorrect standard error, rejects the null hypothesis much too often when the true value of β is zero. We see here (see also Table 1.1) that using the wrong standard error means that we reject the null hypothesis with a probability of about 0.25, instead of the correct 0.05. Thus this particular test is strongly biased. We are eager to reject, and we do not protect H_0 at all.

At the same time the power given by the solid curve (using the wrong standard error) is highest for true but small values of β between zero and 2.5. When the true value of β reaches 2.5 the power function, representing the maximum likelihood estimate (the dotted curve), shows the highest probability of rejecting the null hypothesis. The dashed line, which uses the correct OLS estimate, remains the least powerful in all situations, although it is unbiased (i.e. has the correct value 0.05 if $\beta = 0$).

Overall, the maximum likelihood power function shows the best results. First, it shows a decent alpha level for the probability of committing

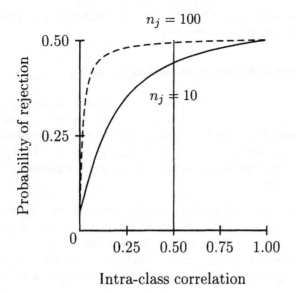

Figure 5.2   Type I error as a function of intra-class correlation

a type 1 error, which is never higher than the acceptable 0.05 level. Second, it shows the highest power by reaching most quickly a probability of 1.00 of rejecting the null hypothesis. Using the correct standard error in OLS lowers the power (we reject less often over the whole range). Maximum likelihood gives us the best of both worlds: no bias and almost perfect power.

When group size is small and intra-class correlation is high, using the wrong OLS standard error causes even more false rejections of the null hypothesis, as is illustrated in more detail in Figure 5.2. In this figure the null hypothesis $\beta = 0$ is true, and we use the test with the wrong standard error V_{OLS}. We plot the probability of wrongly rejecting the null hypothesis, as a function of the intra-class correlation for two group sizes. In Figure 5.2 the intra-class correlation is plotted on the horizontal axis, and the probability of falsely rejecting $\beta = 0$ on the vertical axis (note that for a one-sided test the highest probability of rejection is 0.50). The solid line is for group size $n = 10$, the dashed line for group size $n = 100$. The two curves in Figure 5.2 show the same pattern as the numbers in Table 1.1 in Chapter 1, based on the work of Barcikowski. The alpha level is maximal (and close to 0.50) with values of the intra-class correlation above 0.50, especially when the group size is large. The solid line shows that when group sizes are small ($n = 10$ in our example) the probability of incorrectly rejecting the null hypothesis is lower than when group sizes are large. Figure 5.2 shows that in all cases, using the incorrect standard error leads to too frequent rejection of the true null hypothesis, even for moderate values of the intra-class correlation. It is to be expected that roughly the same results will be found for two-sided testing, and for the situation where we use t-tests when the variance components are estimated.

5.4.2 Review of simulation studies

Monte Carlo simulation is another way to evaluate the power of multilevel modeling. Many different parameters can be studied, and all have their own 'ideal' conditions for maximum power. We can distinguish two broad categories of parameters that are of interest for researchers, the fixed effects (the gammas) and the random effects or variance components (the taus), as summarized below.

- The gamma estimates: the micro-level parameters for slope (γ_{10}), intercept (γ_{00}) and cross-level interaction between micro and macro levels (γ_{11}), the macro parameters for intercept (γ_{01}) and slope (γ_{11}).
- The variance components: micro variance (σ^2), and macro variances for intercept (τ_{00}) and slope (τ_{11}) and the covariance between the two (τ_{01}).

For the gamma estimates, there are, as far as we know, three different simulation studies (Bassiri, 1988; Kim, 1990; Mok, 1995) and two theoretical papers on power (Snijders and Bosker, 1994; Cohen, 1995). Bassiri and Kim report on the power of the gammas under variable intra-class correlations, sample sizes and various numbers of groups. There are two studies that report on the behavior of the variance components in simulation studies with different intra-class correlations and different numbers of groups and observations within groups (Busing, 1993; van der Leeden and Busing, 1994).

The conditions used in Bassiri's study are:

- two different intra-class correlations, 0.10 and 0.25;
- different numbers of groups, between 10 and 150; and
- different numbers of observations within groups, between 5 and 150.

Kim's data replicate a real situation based on the Second International Mathematics Study (SIMS) data. From his simulated data set 50 samples are drawn, over several conditions. Kim's conditions are:

- different relationships in the data – low-magnitude, high-magnitude and mixed-magnitude models;
- different numbers of groups – 25, 50, 100 and 200; and
- different numbers of observations within groups – 10, 20 and 40.

The questions answered by the simulation studies are very similar. Both conclude that the rules are different for first-level estimates than for second-level estimates, and again different for cross-level interactions. To reach an acceptable level of power for first-level parameter estimates the total number of observations is important. The same rules apply as in traditional linear models, with the exception that higher levels of intra-class correlation need to be offset by larger numbers of observations. The power of second-level estimates depends clearly on the number of groups. It is reasonable to ask whether a researcher should collect more groups or collect more individuals within groups. Three papers address this issue. Snijders and Bosker (1994) calculate the trade-off between an increase in the number of groups and the power together with a minimization of cost. They show that it may be many times more costly to collect more groups than more individuals within a group. Two other papers dealing with the same problem, both unfortunately unpublished, are by Cohen (1995) and Mok (1995).

Cohen (1995) takes the costs of sampling an additional school or an additional student within a school into account. He then uses approximate expressions for the standard errors of variance components or regression coefficients to find the optimal number of students per school that should be sampled. It turns out, in most cases, that this number is inversely proportional to the square root of the ratio of the between- and within-variance components. The proportionality factor is determined by the costs.

In Mok (1995), simulation is used to show the following.

> It was found that, consistent with advice given in the classical literature of cluster sampling designs, if resources were available for a sample size n, comprising J schools with I students from each school, then less bias and more efficiency would be expected from sampling design involving more schools (large J), and fewer students per school (small I) than sample design involving fewer schools (small J), and more students per school (large I).

The power to detect cross-level interactions is studied by Bassiri (1988) and van der Leeden and Busing (1994). Both studies show that to obtain sufficient power to detect cross-level interactions at least 30 groups, and 30 observations within each group, are needed. It is also observed that 60 groups, with 25 observations per group (total $n = 1500$), will produce sufficiently high power. With fewer groups, for instance 30, many more observations per group are needed to obtain a power of 0.90. When many groups are present, for example 150, five observations per group will suffice to obtain a power of 0.90, bringing the total number of observations to 750. Using fewer observations (either groups or individuals) leads to a rapid decline of power for the detection of cross-level interactions. To obtain a high power of 0.90, Bassiri finds that collecting data over many groups, instead of over many individuals, produces the most favorable situation for the detection of cross-level interaction effects.

The results of the two simulation studies that report on the behavior of the variance components under different conditions (Busing, 1993; van der Leeden and Busing, 1994) show that irrespective of method (IGLS or RIGLS), the variance components are underestimated or biased downward, while bias is only absent in large data sets with 300 groups. Samples with a small number of groups, for instance 5 and 10, produce widely different values, none including the true value. For the conditions of these studies, see Section 5.6.

5.4.3 Conclusions

The difference in power is based on the error variance of the fixed effects. Our conclusion was that maximum likelihood estimation gives overall the highest power. Since the fixed effects are not affected by estimation methods, but the standard errors are, we conclude that for the fixed estimates the EB/ML estimation method, as employed in multilevel models, has on average the highest power and the lowest probability of making a type I error (see Figures 5.1 and 5.2).

To obtain sufficient power we need, in general, large numbers of observations, unless the effects in the data are very strong and easily detected. The ideal number of observations will differ from situation to situation, and from data to data. When the number of groups is small, the random components are underestimated (in IGLS) or have large standard errors (in RIGLS). Sufficient power for finding cross-level effects can be obtained when groups are not too small, and the number of groups is larger than 20.

Of course results depend very much on the strength of the effect, which is true for all estimates, as well as on the intra-class correlation, which is especially true for second-level estimates and cross-level interactions. At the beginning of this section, we said that it was not easy to answer the general question posed as FAQ 3. Much can be said, but the many different factors that are involved make it hard to state unambiguous conclusions, or even suggest useful rules of thumb. The simulation studies show that the answer is more straightforward for fixed effects than for random effects. For other reasons, such as cost-effectiveness and ease of data collection, the problem of more individual observations versus more groups becomes important, as discussed in the three papers we cited in this section.

5.5 To be or not to be random

Frequently Asked Question 4. A coefficient in a multilevel analysis can be non-random and constant for all groups, it can be non-random and variable over groups, and it can be random (which also means, of course, that it is variable). What does it mean to choose either one of these options, and what are the consequences of changing from one option to another?

We will show that, as usual, the answer is different in different situations. It makes a difference if a random slope is part of the model or if only a random intercept is included in the model. The answer also depends on the relative sizes of the between and within regression coefficients, and on the ratio of the individual-level and group-level variances. Under simplifying conditions we will derive some formulas that make it possible to show that the estimators for the fixed effects change by adding a random intercept and/or random slope. This change can be small or large, depending on the size of the first-level variance σ^2 and the second-level variance τ^2.

5.5.1   ANCOVA versus RANCOVA versus simple regression

We first look at the analysis of covariance, that is to say, at the model

$$y_{ij} = \alpha_j + \beta x_{ij} + \underline{\varepsilon}_{ij}. \tag{5.16}$$

This looks like an ordinary regression model, apart from the subscript j for the intercept, indicating that it is expected to vary among groups. Since intercepts are means (or, in this case, corrected means), it is assumed that means are different. In an ANCOVA model the means are compared. Thus each group has its own intercept, and the intercepts are modeled as fixed, unknown quantities. All groups have the same constant slope β for their regression lines.

The corresponding random coefficient model, which we call RANCOVA, looks very similar, with the difference that the intercept is not only variable, as in equation (5.16), but also random, as indicated by underlining α in equation (5.17) below. This distinction between an intercept that is variable or random is important in a statistical as well as conceptual sense. We write the RANCOVA model as

$$\underline{y}_{ij} = \underline{\alpha}_j + \beta x_{ij} + \underline{\varepsilon}_{ij}, \tag{5.17a}$$

with

$$\underline{\alpha}_j = \alpha + \underline{\delta}_j. \tag{5.17b}$$

The difference between ANCOVA and RANCOVA is, in the first place, at the conceptual level. The α_j in equation (5.16) can be any set of numbers. They can vary wildly, be bimodal, one of them can be very much larger than the others, and so on. In contrast, the $\underline{\alpha}_j$ in equation (5.17a) are assumed to be a random sample from a normal distribution with mean α and variance τ^2. This imposes a certain regularity on them, especially when the number of groups is large.

Also observe that if the group-level variance τ^2 is zero, that is, there is no disturbance term in equation (5.17b), then the RANCOVA model becomes $\underline{y}_{ij} = \alpha + \beta x_{ij} + \underline{\varepsilon}_{ij}$. This defines an ordinary linear regression model, instead of an ANCOVA model, since α is now a constant which does not vary over groups.

In comparing the consequences of (5.16) and (5.17) we see that in ANCOVA there is more structure in the means. The regression lines are parallel straight lines, one line for each group (see Figure 3.1 in Chapter 3). In RANCOVA there is only a single line, but there is more structure in the variances (see Figure 3.4 in Chapter 3). In particular, observations in the same group are correlated. Another way of formulating the distinction is that in ANCOVA we use the means for modeling, while in RANCOVA we rely more on the variances and covariances. These differences are also illustrated in the figures in Sections 3.3 and 3.4 of Chapter 3.[4]

It is of interest to look at the differences between the maximum likelihood estimates of the slope β in the ANCOVA and RANCOVA models. This is done in detail in Longford (1993). We only give a short introduction here.

For completeness we also draw a comparison with the ordinary linear regression model, which has a single variance component σ^2, but which supposes all intercepts α_j to be equal to α. Thus if we go from ordinary regression to ANCOVA we see the effect on the slope of allowing the intercepts to be varying, and if we go to RANCOVA we see the effect of allowing them to be random. All the estimates of β we discuss are weighted means of the between-groups regression coefficient b_B and the within-groups regression coefficient b_W. They are all unbiased, in both the ANCOVA and RANCOVA models.

Our starting point is the classical contextual formula (2.7), which we repeat here:

$$b_T = \eta^2(x)b_B + (1 - \eta^2(x))b_W. \tag{5.18}$$

Remember that $\eta^2(x)$ is the squared intra-class correlation, that is to say, the proportion of variance that is between groups. The formula tells us what happens if we go from simple regression, in which the slope estimate is b_T, to ANCOVA, in which it is b_W. We see that if $\eta^2(x)$ is close to zero, then the total regression coefficient b_T and the within-groups regression coefficient b_W will be approximately equal. This happens if there is very little variation in the group means. Also, if b_B and b_W are approximately equal, then b_T will be close to both b_W and b_B, no matter what $\eta^2(x)$ is.

It can be shown that in the balanced case in RANCOVA, in which all groups are of equal size n, the maximum likelihood estimate satisfies an equation very similar to (5.18). It is more complicated, because it now involves the variance components, but the structure of the formula is exactly the same. Both are weighted averages of b_B and b_W, with non-negative weights that add up to one. The maximum likelihood estimate of the slope is

$$\hat{\beta}_{ML} = \frac{\lambda^2\eta^2(x)}{\lambda^2\eta^2(x) + (1 - \eta^2(x))}b_B + \frac{(1 - \eta^2(x))}{\lambda^2\eta^2(x) + (1 - \eta^2(x))}b_W, \tag{5.19a}$$

where

$$\lambda^2 = \frac{\sigma^2}{\sigma^2 + n\tau^2}. \tag{5.19b}$$

Observe that λ^2 is the ratio of the first-level variance σ^2 and the between-group variance ω^2, discussed in Section 5.3, where we defined it as $\omega^2 = \sigma^2 + n\tau^2$.

The maximum likelihood RANCOVA estimate of beta, $\hat{\beta}_{ML}$, will be between the two extremes b_B and b_W. If all variance is at the first level, then $\lambda^2 = 1$; that is, if the second-level variance $\tau^2 = 0$, then $\hat{\beta}_{ML} = b_T$. This makes sense, because we have just shown that in this case RANCOVA becomes the simple linear model with a fixed intercept α.

If the between variance is very large compared to the first-level variance σ^2, then λ^2 is close to zero, and $\hat{\beta}_{ML}$ will be close to b_W, the ANCOVA estimate. This happens, for example, if the group size is very large, because in that case $n\tau^2$ will be large.

If $\eta^2(x) = 1$, that is to say, if x is a group-level variable and has no within-group variance, then $\hat{\beta} = b_B$; and conversely, if x is group mean centered and has no between-group variance, we see that $\hat{\beta} = b_W$.

Thus the question what will happen to the estimate of the slope if we make the intercept random has the usual, somewhat unsatisfactory, answer. It depends. Let us compare ANCOVA and RANCOVA. If $n\tau^2$ (i.e. either the second-order variance or the group size or both are large), it will not make much difference. In this case λ^2 is close to zero, and thus the weight of b_B in equation (5.19a) will be close to zero. As a result the maximum likelihood estimate in RANCOVA will be close to b_W. Using the same reasoning, if $\eta^2(x)$ is small, it will not make much difference either. For RANCOVA to be different from simple regression, we must have an appreciable difference between $\hat{b}_B$ and $\hat{b}_W$. But even if $\hat{b}_B$ and $\hat{b}_W$ are very different, we can still have $\hat{\beta}_{ML}$ close to b_T if the intercept variance τ^2 is small.

5.5.2 Fixed versus random slopes

If random slopes enter the picture, things are no longer quite so simple. Our FAQ in this case can be formulated as follows. Let us first estimate slopes and intercepts in the submodel in which the variance of the slope is zero, that is, the slope is fixed. Then we estimate the slopes in the model which does not make this additional assumption, that is, we 'make β random'. What happens to the estimates $\hat{\alpha}$ and $\hat{\beta}$ of the intercept and slope?

Let us consider a simple model, with a single explanatory variable,

$$\underline{y}_{ij} = \underline{\alpha}_j + \underline{\beta}_j x_{ij} + \underline{\varepsilon}_{ij}, \qquad (5.20a)$$

where intercept and slope are both random

$$\underline{\alpha}_j = \alpha + \underline{\delta}_{0j}, \qquad (5.20b)$$

$$\underline{\beta}_j = \beta + \underline{\delta}_{1j}. \qquad (5.20c)$$

In order to keep matters simple we assume various conditions that make the design balanced.[5] We assume that all groups have the same size n, that the x_{ij} are expressed as deviations from the group mean, and that the sum of squares s_j of the x_{ij} is the same for all groups too. Moreover, we suppose $\underline{\delta}_{0j}$ and $\underline{\delta}_{1j}$ are uncorrelated, with variances τ_0^2 and τ_1^2. These assumptions may seem somewhat specific, although they do hold in various balanced repeated measures situations. We hope that the results we find will be approximately true in cases in which the assumptions do not hold or hold only approximately.

Under our simplifying assumptions, and after some unpleasant calculations, we find that the maximum likelihood estimate of α is always equal to the corrected mean. Of course, the correction depends on the maximum likelihood estimate of β, which is given by another equation similar to (5.18) and (5.19), in the sense that it gives yet another weighted average of b_B and b_W:

$$\hat{\beta}_{ML} = \frac{\lambda_0^2 \eta^2(x)}{\lambda_0^2 \eta^2(x) + \lambda_1^2(1 - \eta^2(x))} b_B + \frac{\lambda_1^2(1 - \eta^2(x))}{\lambda_0^2 \eta^2(x) + \lambda_1^2(1 - \eta^2(x))} b_W. \quad (5.21a)$$

Here we have two measures of the within–between variance ratio, one (λ_0^2) related to the random intercept and one (λ_1^2) related to the random slope:

$$\lambda_0^2 = \frac{\sigma^2}{\sigma^2 + n\tau_0^2}, \quad (5.21b)$$

$$\lambda_1^2 = \frac{\sigma^2}{\sigma^2 + s\tau_1^2}. \quad (5.21c)$$

Observe that if $\tau_1^2 = 0$, that is, the slope is not random, then the estimate in formula (5.21a) becomes identical to that in Formula (5.19a). By comparing the two we can see what happens if we 'make the slope random'.

The same type of discussion is possible here as in Section 5.5.1. If $\lambda_0^2 \eta^2(x)$ is much smaller than $\lambda_1^2(1 - \eta^2(x))$, then $\hat{\beta}_{ML}$ will be close to b_W. By checking equations (5.21) the reader can easily find out when these products are small and when not.

If λ_0^2 and λ_1^2 are about equal, then $\hat{\beta}_{ML}$ will be close to b_T. If we make the slope random, then the estimated λ_1^2 will decrease. If everything else remains the same, then this means $\hat{\beta}_{ML}$ will become more like b_B.

We can study, along similar lines, what happens to the standard error of the regression coefficients if we 'make them random'. But we have to be very careful here, for the same reasons as in Section 5.4. The standard error depends both on the model we fit and on the model that is true. We can fit a model that is not true, such as a model that fits a fixed slope which is 'really' random. But we can also fit a model with a random slope if the slope is 'really' fixed. Since fixed is a special case of random, this is not really 'wrong'. But we can expect that 'making the slope random' will have quite different effects in both situations.

It will probably not be surprising that things become a bit too complicated if we add more variables, and look at the effect of making one variable random on the regression coefficients of the other variables. In order to study these more complicated model selection choices, we cannot do without matrix algebra, and that would take us beyond what we wish to discuss in this book.

5.6   Estimation techniques and algorithms

Frequently Asked Question 5. What are FIML, REML, EM, IGLS, RIGLS, EB/ML, OLS, GLS?

As indicated in the paper by de Leeuw and Kreft (1995), it is important to distinguish *models*, *techniques* and *algorithms*.

A *model*, more specifically a *statistical model*, consists of a number of equations that describe relationships between random quantities. Remember that random coefficient models deal with fixed predictors, but in the model there is always a random part (indicated by underlining in this book), consisting of the disturbance terms and/or the random coefficients. Models generally have a number of unknown *parameters*, which are used to describe particular *instances* of the model. If our model is a single normally distributed random variable, then the parameters of this model are the mean and variance of the normal distribution. As our discussion of centering in this chapter shows, sometimes the same model (i.e. the same family of random variables) can be described using different *parameterizations*.

A *statistical technique* is a function, or program, that takes the data as input and produces values of the unknown parameters. More generally, a statistical technique transforms the data into a number of statistics. Such statistics can be estimates of model parameters, but they can also be descriptive statistics, or even tables or graphs. Very often, a statistical technique is derived by applying a *statistical principle* to a model. The statistical principle might be maximum likelihood or least squares. A statistical principle is used to associate a technique automatically with a model. If the model is a particular multilevel model, then applying the principle of maximum likelihood tells us to compute maximum likelihood estimates of the parameters of the model.

Techniques are implemented by *algorithms*. Even after we have decided that we must compute maximum likelihood estimates in a given model, we still can use different algorithms to carry out the computations. In fact, if we want to be even more specific, we could argue that even choosing an algorithm does not completely determine what we are going to do. It makes sense in many cases to distinguish different computer programs implementing the same algorithm, in the same way as we distinguish different algorithms implementing the same technique.

With these distinctions in mind, we can now discuss some of the common techniques and algorithms used in multilevel analysis. We have already discussed, in Chapter 1, the many different models and the different computer programs implementing the algorithms.

The dominant principle used by the developers of multilevel techniques is maximum likelihood. Some confusion is possible, however, because one can apply the principle in two slightly different ways. Multilevel models describe the dependent variable $\underline{y}$, and apply the principle of maximum likelihood to this model. The distribution of $\underline{y}$ is assumed to be normal, with a mean depending on the regression coefficients, which are, in the notation used in this book the γ_{st}, and a dispersion depending on the variance components, in our notation ω_{st} and σ^2. These are the parameters that are estimated by the corresponding technique, which is simply called maximum likelihood, but sometimes also *full information maximum likelihood* or FIML.

Alternatively, we can apply the principle of maximum likelihood to the least-squares residuals. This is known as *restricted or residual maximum likelihood*, or REML. It means that we first remove the effect of the fixed variables: remember that the residuals are uncorrelated with all the fixed variables in the model. The distribution of the residuals is also normal, because computing residuals from y just involves taking weighted sums. But the distribution of the residuals no longer depends on the estimates of the fixed effects, the γ_{st}, it only depends on the variance components. Thus applying the maximum likelihood principle to the residuals implies we cannot estimate the regression coefficients. This is somewhat unsatisfactory, and thus we invoke another principle to estimate the regression coefficients. This other principle is *generalized or weighted least squares* (GLS), in which we use the estimated variance components to construct the weight matrix.

Some other principles that are invoked in this context are *Bayes* and especially *empirical Bayes*. In a fully Bayesian approach unknown parameters are thought of as random variables, with a known prior distribution. This makes Bayesian regression quite similar to random coefficient regression. The distribution of the regression coefficients corresponds with the prior distribution. In fully Bayesian statistics we use the prior distribution in Bayes' theorem to compute the posterior distribution of the parameters. This leads to very complicated computations, which are often implemented by using Markov chain Monte Carlo algorithms such as the Gibbs sampler. In empirical Bayes we do not assume that the prior distribution is completely known, but we assume that it depends on a number of unknown parameters that also have to be estimated. Thus this approach is very similar indeed to the random coefficient or multilevel approach; in fact it turns out that empirical Bayes is basically identical to maximum likelihood.

As far as algorithms are concerned, there are many possibilities. HLM (Bryk *et al.*, 1996) uses the EM algorithm to compute its REML estimates, with some special steps to accelerate convergence. The EM algorithm is a general method to compute maximum likelihood estimates in cases in which there are missing data (or random parameters). The special form of the likelihood in such cases suggests a method to approximate the complicated function we are maximizing by a simpler one. In each step we maximize the simpler function, and then we form a new and hopefully better approximation. EM is constructed in such a way that convergence is guaranteed, but often this is painfully slow.

The *Gauss–Newton method*, which is in this context also known as the *method of scoring*, requires much more work per iteration, but because we have faster convergence it needs fewer iterations. The method is based on a better approximation to the likelihood function, and it can be used for both FIML and REML. FIML is used in VARCL (Longford, 1990), while both methods can be used in MLn, where IGLS is used to compute the unrestricted and RIGLS to compute the restricted maximum likelihood estimates. The two last methods are based on the observation that the likelihood function is simple to optimize over the regression coefficients if we know the variance components. And it is also simple to optimize over the variance components if we know the regression coefficients. Thus we alternate these two forms of minimization. First the variance components are guessed, then the optimal corresponding regression coefficients are computed by GLS. Given these regression coefficients, we approximate the likelihood function by a quadratic function of the variance components, and we minimize this by GLS as well, giving us new variance components, and so on.

Understanding the details of the techniques and the algorithms is well beyond the scope of this book. Our hope is that the reader will no longer be overwhelmed by all these acronyms, but also will be able to distinguish clearly between REML and RIGLS, for instance. REML defines a loss function that must be minimized, that is, a statistical technique, while RIGLS defines one way of minimizing that particular loss function.

5.6.1 Which is best, FIML or REML?

The choice between a restricted and an unrestricted estimation method is a matter of some interest – the more so since both methods are available in MLn, where IGLS is used to compute FIML estimates and RIGLS to compute REML estimates. How and why one method is chosen over the other is still unclear. In Bryk and Raudenbush (1992) REML is presented as sometimes superior to FIML, in particular for small data sets, where 'small' means a small number of groups rather than a small number of observations per group. Remember that REML (or RIGLS for that matter) starts the calculation based on the residuals after the fixed effects are estimated. Goldstein (1995) discusses the two methods in his book, but does not give precise directions as to which method to use in which situation. That leaves us with only one source of information, simulation studies. From these studies we learn that over all estimation methods the most important requirement for the estimation of the variance components is to have a large number of groups.

Since Monte Carlo simulation is a way to evaluate the statistical properties of multilevel estimation methods, we report here the results obtained from several such studies.

The studies are based on many replications of artificial data sets with known parameters, and are by no means exhaustive. Most use low intra-class correlations ($r \leq 0.25$), which makes the results most relevant for social and educational research. Two simulation studies examine the behavior of the fixed parameter estimates, the gammas (Kim, 1990; van der Leeden and Busing, 1994), and two examine the behavior of the variance components under different estimation methods (Busing, 1993; van der Leeden and Busing, 1994). The conditions of the last two studies are described in Section 5.6.3, while for the conditions of Kim's study we refer to Section 5.4.2.

5.6.2 The effect of estimation methods on the fixed coefficients

The estimation methods compared by Kim are OLS, GLS and EB/ML (in the form of REML). His results show that the estimates behave in the same way under all conditions of the study. He also shows that to obtain unbiased estimates it is not necessary to use a complicated EB/ML method. All three methods give unbiased fixed parameter estimates.

We recalculated the efficiency of the fixed parameter estimates of Kim's study, again comparing the three different estimation methods, OLS, GLS and REML. We found that the precision of the gamma estimates is the same for GLS and REML. Small differences are found between the precision of OLS and REML, indicated by a somewhat larger variance of the estimates in OLS. This is no longer true for large data sets, where no difference is found between OLS and the other two methods in the efficiency of the gamma parameters. OLS efficiency is about 90% over all conditions in Kim's data. This lower efficiency means that more observations are needed to obtain the same efficiency as obtained by GLS and REML. The overall conclusions regarding the gammas are:

- GLS produces optimal solutions for the fixed parameters in the random coefficient model;
- the OLS starting values of the random coefficient software are slightly less efficient;
- GLS and EB/ML are equally efficient; and
- the gamma estimates are unbiased for all estimation methods.

Van der Leeden and Busing (1994) also compare the three estimation methods for the values of the cross-level estimates. The methods are OLS, GLS and RIGLS (equivalent to REML in HLM). They observed, as did Kim's study, no difference between the OLS, GLS and IGLS estimates for the cross-level estimates of gamma under several conditions. All three methods produced unbiased estimates.

5.6.3   Estimation methods for variance components

Busing (1993) and van der Leeden and Busing (1994) study the behavior of variance components. The former studies the behavior of variance components estimated by an unrestricted method (IGLS). The latter study reports the results of a restricted estimation method (RIGLS). Both studies use the MLn program (Rasbash et al., 1990) to estimate the parameters. The estimation methods are compared in relation to sample size, intra-class correlation, and number of groups under the following conditions:

- intra-class correlations of 0.20, 0.40, 0.60 and 0.80;
- correlations between intercept and slopes of 0.25, 0.50 and 0.75;
- sample sizes – all combinations of the following numbers of groups and of observations within groups;
- numbers of groups – 5, 10, 25, 50, 100, 300;
- numbers of observations within groups – 5, 10, 25, 50, 100;
- results regarding relative bias of variance components for slope, intercept, and their covariances, and relative bias of standard errors;

- 1000 replications for each condition.

Comparing the IGLS and RIGLS results for the variance components shows differences. RIGLS is less biased but also less efficient than IGLS, which makes it hard to choose between the two methods. The trade-off between them is complicated and the pattern over the different conditions in the study is very irregular. The authors of these studies were unable to give a clear indication of when to use RIGLS and when to use IGLS, or equivalently when to use REML and when to use FIML.

The two studies report that the GLS estimates of the variance components, which are obtained after one iteration, show a lower precision than the estimates obtained after convergence is reached. The variance component for the intercept is estimated with increased precision over iterations, while the mean squared error decreases with the number of iterations, for both IGLS and RIGLS. In contrast to the conclusions reached for the fixed effects, iterations do indeed improve estimation of the random effects.

5.6.4 Conclusions

Simulation studies show that the fixed effects are equally unbiased in all estimation methods – OLS, GLS and REML. A difference observed among the methods is in the efficiency of the fixed parameter estimates. The OLS method is less efficient (but still unbiased) for all but large data sets. For the variance components it is not yet clear which method to use. The pattern observed is that the advantage of RIGLS over IGLS of less bias is offset by the disadvantage of less precision in RIGLS.

5.7 Multicollinearity

Frequently Asked Question 6. How serious is the problem of multicollinearity in multilevel analysis?

In classical regression analysis a great deal of attention is paid to *multicollinearity*. A thorough review has been done by Belsley (1991). There are some interesting multicollinearity issues that are particularly important in multilevel analysis. In a full-blown multilevel analysis we have three types of regressor: first-level variables, second-level variables and cross-level interactions (which are products of first-level and second-level variables). All variables can be written as the sum of a between-group and a within-group component, as in

$$x_{ij} = x_{\bullet j} + (x_{ij} - x_{\bullet j}). \tag{5.22}$$

The two components, the group mean $x_{\bullet j}$ and the deviation score $x_{ij} - x_{\bullet j}$ are uncorrelated. For second-level variables the within-group component is zero. For first-level variables expressed as deviations from the group mean the between-group component is zero. If variables are expressed as deviations from the group mean, they are uncorrelated with all second-level variables. Moreover, if a first-level variable is expressed in terms of deviation from the group mean, then the cross-level interactions of this variable with any second-level variable are uncorrelated.

It is interesting to find out what happens if we add a cross-level interaction to our multilevel model. We have seen in Chapter 4 that such an interaction often surpresses the first-level main effect and causes various forms of instability.

If we ignore, for the moment, that we are dealing with multilevel models with more than one variance component, we can use the general theory of *added variables* to find out the effect of adding a cross-level interaction (Weisberg, 1985, Section 2.4).

The added-variable theory gives us the following recipe. Suppose we have performed a regression with a number of predictors $x_1, \ldots, x_p$ and we add an additional predictor z. Two questions spring to mind.

- How does $\beta_1, \ldots, \beta_p$ change if we add z to the regression?
- What is the regression coefficient γ of z?

There is a simple recipe for answering the first question. We regress y on z, and compute the residuals $\tilde{y}$. We also regress each of the x_s on z and compute the residuals $\tilde{x}_s$. We then compute $\tilde{\beta}_1, \ldots, \tilde{\beta}_p$ by regressing $\tilde{y}$ on $\tilde{x}_1, \ldots, \tilde{x}_p$. This $\tilde{\beta}$ is equal to the new β we get for $\tilde{x}_1, \ldots, \tilde{x}_p$ if we add z to the regression. If z is a cross-level interaction, this means we remove the cross-level interaction from both the first-level and second-level predictors before we do the new regression. Clearly if the correlation between z and one of the x_s is high, then we will remove almost all variation from that x_s, and the corresponding β will change a great deal.

The second question can be answered using a similar recipe. In order to compute the coefficient γ of the added variable z we can first regress y on $\tilde{x}_1, \ldots, \tilde{x}_p$ and compute the residuals $y^\dagger$. We can then regress z on the $\tilde{x}_1, \ldots, \tilde{x}_p$ and compute the residuals $z^\dagger$. Then we compute γ by regressing $y^\dagger$ on $z^\dagger$. If z is a cross-level interaction, this means we remove both the first-level and the second-level variable that define z, before computing its regression coefficient. It makes sense to suppose that almost nothing of z will be left after doing this, and thus the regression coefficient of z will tend to be very unstable.

Of course, as usual, in a multilevel analysis with more than one variance component, the situation is less simple. We have seen a number of examples in Chapter 4, but a precise mathematical description is quite complicated, especially because a cross-level interaction is usually associated with a random slope. Thus we will merely illustrate the discussion above with a small example of the correlation coefficients.

In the full NELS-88 data set we select the variables 'HomeWork' and 'SES'. We then compute the aggregated versions 'MeanHomeWork' and 'MeanSES'. Just for the purposes of this section, we will use H and S for 'HomeWork' and 'SES', and $\overline{H}$ and $\overline{S}$ for 'MeanHomeWork' and

Table 5.3 Correlations between first-level variables, second-level variables and cross-level interactions (raw scores below diagonal, centered-within-group scores above diagonal)

	H	S	$\overline{H}$	$\overline{S}$	$\overline{H}H$	$\overline{H}S$	$\overline{S}H$	$\overline{S}S$	M
H	•	0.11	0.00	0.00	0.97	0.12	0.05	−0.01	0.19
S	0.21	•	0.00	0.00	0.11	0.97	−0.01	−0.19	0.25
$\overline{H}$	0.38	0.34	•	0.52	0.00	0.00	0.00	0.00	0.30
$\overline{S}$	0.20	0.65	0.52	•	0.00	0.00	0.00	0.00	0.45
$\overline{H}H$	0.93	0.28	0.63	0.34	•	0.12	0.18	−0.00	0.18
$\overline{H}S$	0.23	0.96	0.39	0.66	0.33	•	−0.00	−0.06	0.24
$\overline{S}H$	0.21	0.52	0.48	0.81	0.40	0.59	•	0.07	0.01
$\overline{S}S$	0.07	0.02	0.21	0.18	0.16	0.19	0.29	•	−0.04
M	0.29	0.48	0.30	0.45	0.33	0.47	0.37	0.07	•

'MeanSES'. Thus we can write the four cross-level interactions as $\overline{H}H$, $\overline{H}S$, $\overline{S}H$, and $\overline{S}S$. We add the variable 'MathAchievement', here simply M, which is the dependent variable in our regressions.

The correlation matrix between these nine variables is given in Table 5.3. Below the diagonal we use H and S in raw score format, while above the diagonal H and S take the form of deviations from the group means. Above the diagonal we see correlations which are generally much smaller, and many of them are actually zero or close to zero. This indicates that there will not be much multicollinearity if our first-level variables are deviations from the group mean. We also see some very high correlations, for instance between H and $\overline{H}H$ and between S and $\overline{H}S$. This is because almost all the variation in homework H is within schools. Thus the mean homework $\overline{H}$ is about the same for all schools, and the cross-level interactions with mean homework $\overline{H}H$ and $\overline{H}S$ will be almost the same as the original first-level variables H and S. Thus regression coefficients in a model with S and $\overline{H}S$ will be very unstable. This is true in raw score models as well as in group centered models. S has much more between-school variation, and thus $\overline{S}H$ is quite different from H, and much more like $\overline{S}$.

Two conclusions seem to follow from the analysis of the correlation coefficients. First, even in fixed coefficient models, the use of cross-level interactions is very problematic. In raw score models, and even in group centered models, it may lead to instabilities. But overall, group mean centering seems to improve the multicollinearity situation considerably. Correlations between second-level variables and both first-level variables and cross-level interactions are exactly zero, which means we only have to worry about correlations between cross-level interactions and the corresponding first-level variables.

Notes

1 At multilevel@mailbase.ac.uk. One subscribes by sending the message 'join multilevel your name' to mailbase@mailbase.ac.uk, and if one has subscribed one can post queries and

`    ` messages to the list. Compare also the World Wide Web homepage at http://www.ioe.ac.uk/ multilevel/, with mirrors at http://www.medent.umontreal.ca/multilevel/ and http://www. edfac.unimelb.edu.au/multilevel/.

2   Suppose the regression is $\alpha + \beta x$, and we add a constant c to x. Then the intercept changes to $\alpha - \beta c$. This is a consequence of the simple identity $\alpha + \beta x = (\alpha - \beta c) + \beta(x + c)$.

3   Following Snijders and Bosker (1994) we will use 'modeled variance' from here onward to avoid unpleasant causal connotations.

4   This is a good place to recall a possible source of confusion, already mentioned in Section 3.9. In RANCOVA we have the basic parameter τ^2, the parameter variance of the random intercepts $\underline{\alpha}_j$. This is the variance of the intercepts over independent replications of the experiment, and we assume all intercepts have the same variance. In ANCOVA there is no intercept variance in the model, but of course we can compute the variance of the m fixed intercepts α_j, which certainly indicates how variable the intercepts are. Finally, we can compute the variance of the m ANCOVA estimates $\hat{\alpha}_j$. All these variance quantities are related, but far from identical. This illustrates that it is critically important to distinguish properties of the model from properties of the estimates.

5   Many of the results can be derived under more general conditions, but they either look more complicated or require matrix calculus.

Appendix CODING OF NELS-88 DATA

SEX COMPOSITE SEX

Label	Code	Freq	Prop
Male	1	10564	0.49
Female.	2	11016	0.51

RACE COMPOSITE RACE

Label	Code	Freq	Prop
Asian or Pacific Islander	1	1277	0.06
Hispanic, regardless of race.	2	2633	0.12
Black, not of Hispanic origin.	3	2480	0.11
White, not of Hispanic origin.	4	14933	0.69
American Indian or Alaskan Native.	5	257	0.01

BYS79A TIME SPENT ON MATH HOMEWORK EACH WEEK

Label	Code	Freq	Prop
None.	0	1779	0.08
Less than 1 hour.	1	8949	0.41
1 hour	2	4942	0.23
2 hours	3	2285	0.11
3 hours	4	1653	0.08
4–6 hours.	5	1563	0.07
7–9 hours.	6	262	0.01
10 or more	7	147	0.01

G8CTRL SCHOOL CONTROL COMPOSITE

Label	Code	Freq	Prop
Public school.	1	16952	0.79
Catholic school	2	2327	0.11
Private, Other Religious Affiliation . .	3	944	0.04
Private, No Religious Affiliation	4	1357	0.06

BYSES SOCIO-ECONOMIC STATUS COMPOSITE

Mean	−0.04
Variance	0.63

BYPARED   PARENTS' HIGHEST EDUCATION LEVEL

Label	Code	Freq	Prop
Did not finish H.S..............	1	2116	0.10
H.S. grad or GED..............	2	4099	0.19
GT H.S. & LT 4yr degree.........	3	8627	0.40
College graduate	4	3341	0.15
M.A. or equivalent	5	2086	0.10
Ph.D., M.D., other	6	1311	0.06

BYTXMNR   MATHEMATICS NUMBER RIGHT

Mean	51.01
Variance	103.72

BYSC47D   CLASSROOM ENVIRONMENT IS STRUCTURED

Label	Code	Freq	Prop
Not at all accurate	1	213	0.01
	2	439	0.02
	3	2360	0.11
	4	10588	0.49
Very much accurate	5	7980	0.37

BYSCENRL   TOTAL SCHOOL ENROLLMENT COMPOSITE

Label	Code	Freq	Prop
1–199 students................	1	1045	0.05
200–399	2	4331	0.20
400–599	3	5404	0.25
600–799	4	4666	0.22
800–999	5	2911	0.13
1000–1199....................	6	1584	0.07
1200+	7	1639	0.08

G8URBAN   URBANICITY COMPOSITE

Label	Code	Freq	Prop
Urban.......................	1	6500	0.30
Suburban	2	8998	0.42
Rural	3	6082	0.28

G8REGON   COMPOSITE GEOGRAPHIC REGION OF SCHOOL

Label	Code	Freq	Prop
NORTHEAST...................	1	4246	0.20
NORTH CENTRAL	2	5659	0.26
SOUTH.......................	3	7470	0.35
WEST	4	4205	0.19

G8MINOR   PERCENT MINORITY IN SCHOOL

Label	Code	Freq	Prop
None.........................	0	2760	0.13
1–5%	1	4905	0.23
6–10%	2	2478	0.11
11–20%	3	2928	0.14
21–40%	4	3173	0.15
41–60%	5	1879	0.09
61–90%	6	1943	0.09
91–100%	7	1514	0.07

BYRATIO   COMPOSITE STUDENT-TEACHER RATIO

Label	Code	Freq	Prop
10 and below..................	10	1451	0.07
	11	780	0.04
	12	599	0.03
	13	1514	0.07
	14	1665	0.08
	15	1895	0.09
	16	2002	0.09
	17	1486	0.07
	18	1924	0.09
	19	1423	0.07
	20	1073	0.05
	21	1161	0.05
	22	800	0.04
	23	1009	0.05
	24	522	0.02
	25	523	0.02
	26	455	0.02
	27	241	0.01
	28	294	0.01
	29	239	0.01
	30	524	0.02

REFERENCES

Aiken, L. S. and West, S. G. (1991) *Multiple Regression: Testing and Interpreting Interaction.* Sage Publications, Newbury Park, CA.

Airy, G. B. (1861) *On the Algebraical and Numerical Theory of Errors of Observations and the Combination of Observations.* Macmillan, London.

Aitkin, M. A. and Longford, N. T. (1986) Statistical modeling issues in school effectiveness studies. *Journal of the Royal Statistical Society A*, **149**, 1–43.

Barcikowski, R. S. (1981) Statistical power with group mean as the unit of analysis. *Journal of Educational Statistics*, **6**(3), 267–85.

Baron, R. M. and Kenny, D. A. (1986) The moderator-mediator variable distinction in social psychological research: Conceptual, strategic, and statistical considerations. *Journal of Personality and Social Psychology*, **51**, 1173–82.

Bassiri, D. (1988) Large and small sample properties of maximum likelihood estimates for the hierarchical linear model. Ph.D. thesis, Department of Counseling, Educational Psychology and Special Education, Michigan State University.

Belsley, D. A. (1991) *Conditioning Diagnostics.* Wiley, New York.

Beran, R. and Hall, P. (1992) Estimating coefficient distributions in random coefficient regressions. *Annals of Statistics*, **20**, 1970–84.

Boyd, L. H. and Iversen, G. R. (1979) *Contextual Analysis: Concepts and Statistical Techniques.* Wadsworth, Belmont, CA.

Bryk, A. S. and Raudenbush, S. W. (1992) *Hierarchical Linear Models: Applications and Data Analysis Methods.* Sage Publications, Newbury Park, CA.

Bryk, A. S., Raudenbush, S. W., Seltzer, M., and Congdon, R. T. (1988) *An Introduction to HLM: Computer Program and User's Guide.* University of Chicago.

Bryk, A. S., Raudenbush, S. W., and Congdon, R. T. (1996) *HLM. Hierarchical Linear and Nonlinear Modeling with the HLM/2L and HLM/3L Programs.* Scientific Software International, Chicago.

Burstein, L. (1980) The analysis of multilevel data in educational research and evaluation. *Review of Research in Education*, **8**, 158–233.

Burstein, L., Linn, R. L., and Capell, F. J. (1978) Analyzing multilevel data in the presence of heterogeneous within-class regressions. *Journal of Educational Statistics*, **3**, 347–83.

Burstein, L., Kim, K.-S., and Delandshere, G. (1989) Multilevel investigation of systematically varying slopes: Issues, alternatives, and consequences. In R. D. Bock (ed.), *Multilevel Analysis of Educational Data.* Academic Press, New York.

Busing, F. M. T. A. (1993) Distribution characteristics of variance estimates in two-level models. Preprint PRM 93-04. Psychometrics and Research Methodology, Leiden, Netherlands.

Chamberlain, G. (1984) Panel data. In Z. Griliches and M. D. Intriligator (eds), *HandBook of Econometrics, Volume 2.* North-Holland, Amsterdam.

Chow, G. C. (1984) Random and changing coefficient models. In Z. Griliches and M. D. Intriligator (eds), *HandBook of Econometrics, Volume 2.* North-Holland, Amsterdam.

Cochran, W. G. (1977) *Sampling Techniques.* Wiley, New York.

Cohen, M. P. (1995) Sample sizes for survey data analyzed with hierarchical linear models. National Center of Education Statistics, Washington, DC.

Coleman, J., Hoffer, T., and Kilgore, S. (1982) Cognitive outcomes in public and private schools. *Sociology of Education*, **55**, 162–82.

Cressie, N. A. C. (1991) *Statistics for Spatial Data*. Wiley, New York.

Cronbach, L. J. and Webb, N. (1975) Between class and within class effects in a reported aptitude × treatment interaction: A reanalysis of a study by G. L. Anderson. *Journal of Educational Psychology*, **67**, 717–24.

Davidian, M. and Gallant, A. R. (1992) *NLMIX: A Program for Maximum Likelihood Estimation of the Nonlinear Mixed Effects Model with a Smooth Random Effects Density*. Department of Statistics, North Carolina State University, Raleigh, NC.

de Leeuw, J. (1994) Statistics and the sciences. In I. Borg and P. Mohler (eds), *Trends and Perspectives in Empirical Social Research*, pp. 139–48. Walter de Gruyter, Berlin.

de Leeuw, J. and Kreft, I. G. G. (1986) Random coefficient models for multilevel analysis. *Journal of Educational Statistics*, **11**, 57–86.

de Leeuw, J. and Kreft, I. G. G. (1995) Questioning multilevel models. *Journal of Educational and Behavioral Statistics*, **20**, 171–90.

Dielman, T. E. (1992) *Pooled Cross-Sectional and Time Series Data Analysis*. Marcel Dekker, New York.

Diggle, P. J., Liang, K.-Y., and Zeger, S. L. (1994) *Analysis of Longitudinal Data*. Clarendon Press, Oxford.

Draper, D. (1995) Inference and hierarchical modeling in the social sciences. *Journal of Educational and Behavioral Statistics*, **20**(2), 115–47.

Duncan, O. D., Curzort, R. P., and Duncan, R. P. (1966) *Statistical Geography: Problems in Analyzing Areal Data*. Free Press, Glencoe, IL.

Efron, B. and Morris, C. N. (1975) Data analysis using Stein's estimator and its generalizations. *Journal of the American Statistical Association*, **74**, 311–19.

Eisenhart, C. (1947) The assumptions underlying the analysis of variance. *Biometrics*, **3**, 1–21.

Engel, B. (1990) The analysis of the unbalanced linear models with variance components. *Statistica Neerlandica*, **44**, 195–219.

Fisher, R. A. (1918) The correlation between relatives on the supposition of Mendelian inheritance. *Transactions of the Royal Society of Edinburgh*, **52**, 399–433.

Fisher, R. A. (1925) *Statistical Methods for Research Workers*. Oliver and Boyd, Edinburgh and London.

Geisser, S. (1980) Growth curve analysis. In P. R. Krishnaiah (ed.), *HandBook of Statistics, Volume 1*. North-Holland, Amsterdam.

Goldstein, H. (1987) *Multilevel Models in Educational and Social Research*. Griffin, London.

Goldstein, H. (1995) *Multilevel Statistical Models*. Edward Arnold, London.

Hartley, H. O. and Rao, J. N. K. (1967) Maximum likelihood estimation for the mixed analysis of variance model. *Biometrika*, **54**, 93–108.

Harville, D. A. (1977) Maximum-likelihood approaches to variance component estimation and to related problems. *Journal of the American Statistical Association*, **72**, 320–40.

Hastie, T. and Tibshirani, R. (1990) *Generalized Additive Models*. Chapman & Hall, London.

Hastie, T. and Tibshirani, R. (1993) Varying coefficient models (with discussion). *Journal of the Royal Statistical Society B*, **55**, 757–96.

Hedeker, D. (1989) Random regression models with autocorrelated errors. Ph.D. thesis, University of Chicago.

Hedeker, D. and Gibbons, R. (1993a) *MIXOR. A Computer Program for Mixed-Effects Ordinal Probit and Logistic Regression Analysis.* University of Illinois at Chicago.

Hedeker, D. and Gibbons, R. (1993b) *MIXREG. A Computer Program for Mixed-Effects Regression Analysis with Autocorrelated Errors.* University of Illinois at Chicago.

Hedeker, D. and Gibbons, R. D. (1994) A random effects ordinal regression model for multilevel analysis. *Biometrics,* **50**, 933–44.

Hemelrijk, J. (1966) Underlining random variables. *Statistica Neerlandica,* **20**, 1–7.

Hemmerle, W. J. and Hartley, H. O. (1973) Computing maximum likelihood estimates for the mixed A.O.V. model using the W-transformation. *Technometrics,* **15**, 819–31.

Henderson, C. R. (1953) Estimation of variance and covariance components. *Biometrics,* **9**, 226–52.

Hsiao, C. (1986) *Analysis of Panel Data.* Cambridge University Press, Cambridge.

Jennrich, R. and Schluchter, M. (1986) Unbalanced repeated measures models with structured covariance matrices. *Biometrics,* **42**, 805–20.

Johnson, L. W. (1977) Stochastic parameter regression: an annotated bibliography. *International Statistical Review,* **45**, 257–72.

Johnson, L. W. (1980) Stochastic parameter regression: an additional annotated bibliography. *International Statistical Review,* **48**, 95–102.

Kim, K.-S. (1990) Multilevel data analysis: A comparison of analytical alternatives. Ph.D. thesis, University of California, Los Angeles.

Kreft, I. G. G. (1994) Multilevel models for hierarchically nested data: Potential applications in substance abuse prevention research. In L. M. Collins and L. A. Seitz (eds), *Advances in Data Analysis for Prevention Intervention Research.* Research Monograph 108. National Institute on Drug Abuse, Washington, DC.

Kreft, I. G. G., de Leeuw, J., and Kim, K.-S. (1990) Comparing four different statistical packages for hierarchical linear regression: Genmod, HLM, ML2, VARCL. Preprint 50. UCLA Statistics, Los Angeles, CA.

Kreft, I. G. G., de Leeuw, J., and van der Leeden, R. (1994) Review of five multilevel analysis programs: BMDP-5V, GENMOD, HLM, ML3, VARCL. *American Statistician,* **48**, 324–35.

Kreft, I. G. G., de Leeuw, J., and Aiken, L. (1995) The effect of different forms of centering in hierarchical linear models. *Multivariate Behavioral Research,* **30**, 1–22.

Lazarsfeld, P. F. and Menzel, H. (1969) On the relation between individual and collective properties. In A. Etzioni (ed.), *A Sociological Reader on Complex Organizations,* pp. 499–516. Holt, Rinehart & Winston, New York.

Lindley, D. V. and Smith, A. F. M. (1972) Bayes estimates for the linear model. *Journal of the Royal Statistical Society B,* **34**, 1–41.

Lindsey, J. K. (1993) *Models for Repeated Measurements.* Clarendon Press, Oxford.

Longford, N. (1993) *Random Coefficient Models.* Oxford University Press, Oxford.

Longford, N. T. (1990) *VARCL. Software for Variance Component Analysis of Data with Nested Random Effects (Maximum Likelihood).* Educational Testing Service, Princeton, NJ.

McMillan, N. J. and Berliner, M. J. (1994) A spatially correlated hierarchical random effect model for Ohio corn yield. Technical Report 10. National Institute for Statistical Sciences, Research Triangle Park, NC.

Mok, M. (1995) Sample size requirements for 2-level designs in educational research. Macquarie University, Sydney, Australia.

Morris, C. N. (1983) Parametric empirical Bayes inference: Theory and applications. *Journal of the American Statistical Association*, **78**, 47–65.

National Research Council (1992) *Combining Information. Statistical Issues and Opportunities for Research*. National Academy Press, Washington, DC.

Pothoff, R. F. and Roy, S. N. (1964) A generalized multivariate analysis of variance model useful especially for growth curve problems. *Biometrika*, **51**, 313–26.

Prosser, R., Rasbash, J., and Goldstein, H. (1991) Data analysis with ML3. Technical report. Institute of Education, University of London.

Rao, C. R. (1965) The theory of least squares when parameters are stochastic and its application to the analysis of growth curves. *Biometrika*, **52**, 447–58.

Rasbash, J. and Woodhouse, G. (1995) *MLn Command Reference*. Institute of Education, University of London.

Rasbash, J., Prosser, R., and Goldstein, H. (1990) *ML3. Software for Three-Level Analysis. User's Guide*. Institute of Education, University of London.

Rasbash, J., Prosser, R., and Goldstein, H. (1991) *ML3. Software for Three-Level Analysis. User's Guide for V-2*. Institute of Education, University of London.

Raudenbush, S. W. and Bryk, A. S. (1986) A hierarchical model for studying school effects. *Sociology of Education*, **59**, 1–17.

Robinson, W. S. (1950) Ecological correlations and the behavior of individuals. *Sociological Review*, **15**, 351–7.

Rosenberg, B. (1973) A survey of stochastic parameter regression. *Annals of Economic and Social Measurement*, **2**, 381–97.

Rubin, H. (1950) Note on random coefficients. In T. C. Koopmans (ed.), *Statistical Inference in Dynamic Economic Models*. Wiley, New York.

Samuels, M. L., Casella, G., and McCabe, G. P. (1991) Interpreting blocks and random factors (with discussion). *Journal of the American Statistical Association*, **86**, 798–821.

Saunders, D. R. (1956) Moderator variables in prediction. *Educational and Psychological Measurement*, **16**, 209–22.

Scheffé, H. (1956) Alternative models for the analysis of variance. *Annals of Mathematical Statistics*, **27**, 251–71.

Searle, S. R. (1979) Notes on variance components estimation. A detailed account of maximum likelihood and kindred methodology. Technical report BU-673-M, Biometrics Unit, Cornell University, Ithaca, NY.

Searle, S. R., Casella, G., and McCulloch, C. E. (1992) *Variance Components*. Wiley, New York.

Smith, A. F. M. (1973) A general Bayesian linear model. *Journal of the Royal Statistical Society B*, **35**, 67–75.

Snijders, T. A. B. and Bosker, R. J. (1994) Modeled variance in two-level models. *Sociological Methods and Research*, **22**, 342–63.

Speed, T. P. (1987) What is an analysis of variance? (with discussion). *Annals of Statistics*, **15**, 885–941.

Spjøtvoll, E. (1977) Random coefficients regression models. A review. *Mathematische Operationsforschung und Statistik*, **8**, 69–93.

Strenio, J. L. F., Weisberg, H. I., and Bryk, A. S. (1983) Empirical Bayes estimation of individual growth curve parameters and their relationship to covariates. *Biometrics*, **39**, 71–86.

Swamy, P. A. V. B. (1971) *Statistical Inference in a Random Coefficient Model*. Springer-Verlag, New York.

Tate, R. (1985) Methodological observations on applied behavioral science. *Journal of Applied Behavioral Science*, **21**(2), 221–34.

Thomson, R. (1980) Maximum likelihood estimation of variance components. *Mathematische Operationsforschung und Statistik, Serie Statistik*, **11**, 545–61.

Timm, N. H. (1980) Multivariate analysis of variance of repeated measurements. In P. R. Krishnaiah (ed.), *HandBook of Statistics, Volume 1*. North-Holland, Amsterdam.

van der Leeden, R. and Busing, F. M. T. A. (1994) First iteration versus IGLS/RIGLS estimates in two-level models: a Monte Carlo study with ML3. Preprint PRM 94-03. Psychometrics and Research Methodology, Leiden, Netherlands.

Velicer, W. F. (1972) The moderator variable viewed as heterogeneous regression. *Journal of Applied Psychology*, **56**, 266–9.

Wald, A. (1947) A note on regressions analysis. *Annals of Mathematical Statistics*, **18**, 586–9.

Wansbeek, T. J. (1980) Quantitative effects in panel data modelling. Ph.D. thesis, University of Leiden.

Weisberg, S. (1985) *Applied Linear Regression* (second edition). Wiley, New York.

Wilk, M. B. and Kempthorne, O. (1955) Fixed, mixed, and random models. *Journal of the American Statistical Association*, **50**, 1144–67.

Woodhouse, G. (1995) *A Guide to MLn for New Users*. Institute of Education, University of London.

Index